LOUISE DE MARILLAC

LOUISE
DE MARILLAC

A PORTRAIT

by

J. CALVET

Translated by G. F. PULLEN

P. J. KENEDY & SONS

New York

Nihil Obstat: Johannes M. T. Barton, S.T.D., L.S.S.
Imprimatur: E. Morragh Bernard,
Vic. Gen.
Westmonasterii, die 30a Julii, 1959.

This book was first published in France, under the title LOUISE DE MARILLAC PAR ELLE-MÊME, by les Editions Montaigne in 1958.

Printed in Great Britain by the Ditchling Press, Ditchling, Sussex

CONTENTS

INTRODUCTION

SOME SAINTS, although they lived perhaps centuries ago, are well known to us. Others are bound up inseparably with a great achievement in the Church in connection with which their names have become household words; it is impossible to think of theology, for example, without coupling it with the name of St Thomas Aquinas, or the apostolate among working-class boys without at once bringing to mind the name of St John Bosco. The corporal works of mercy, charitable undertakings of all sorts have, ever since the seventeenth century, been almost synonomous with the name of Vincent de Paul, which is perpetuated to this day by the Congregation of the Mission (the Vincentian Fathers) and the Sisters of Charity of St Vincent de Paul, founded by him, whose distinctive habit is known the world over. It is right that the Sisters of Charity should bear his name, for his was the first conception, his was the guiding hand through the first difficult years, his the heavy work and responsibility attending the foundation of any great undertaking—especially one so novel as the Sisters of Charity in the century in which they came into being—to fill a need in the life of the Church.

Yet right as it is that Vincent de Paul's name should be held in honour in this connection, nevertheless one result has been that the name of the woman who was his right hand in the work has been largely overshadowed by his. How many who know the Sisters of Charity connect with them the name of St Louise de Marillac, the first to wear their habit, more than that indeed, their foundress and their mother?

Mgr Calvet's *Portrait* of Louise de Marillac shows her against the background of her times. He has already written

7

the biography of St Vincent de Paul, a huge canvas which
portrays Vincent, the man and the saint, as a national figure
involved in all sorts of enterprises and affairs of state, but
ever concerned first with the many undertakings of 'his
charitable heart'. This later book is also a lifelike portrait,
but it is rather a miniature and so it has the advantage that
we can examine its subject's moral physiognomy, for all the
features are painted in with deftness and clarity.

It is an unusual story that Mgr Calvet has to tell of the
illegitimate daughter of an important family who became a
saint. We follow her through the difficulties of her early
years, increased by the death of her father when she was in
her teens, and see her torn between her desire to become a
Capuchin nun, with all the austerity that such a life would
involve and the impossibility of realising her project on
account of her poor health, and then as the wife of Antony
Le Gras experiencing a married woman's trials with a sick
husband on her hands whom she nursed devotedly.

On her husband's death in 1625 she came increasingly
under Vincent's influence (she had first met him while her
husband was alive) and under his direction was led gradually
to organise charitable undertakings that he had founded to
cope with a problem that was acute. The destitution resulting
from the incessant wars, the care of orphans and foundlings
and much else besides form part of the great charitable
achievement of the seventeenth century that was Vincent de
Paul's, and under him Louise de Marillac's.

Three things emerge very clearly from this admirable life-
story. The first is the novel nature of the experiment undertaken by the two saints. In the seventeenth century the
religious life for women meant a convent and enclosure
together with solemn vows, and two previous attempts to
found congregations of religious women without these safeguards had failed. Not very long beforehand St Angela Merici
(1474-1540), the foundress of the Ursuline nuns, desired to
inaugurate a congregation of women without habit, vows

or other distinctive sign, to teach girls in their own homes; under the influences of St Charles Borromeo and subsequent papal legislation she was obliged to adopt the canonical safeguards then required of all nuns. St Francis de Sales, a near contemporary of Louise's, with the collaboration of St Joan Fremiot de Chantal, similarly intended the first Visitation nuns to be without enclosure, but was overruled. When Vincent and Louise, therefore, founded the Sisters of Charity as religious women without distinctive habit (they wore the peasant costume of their day) or enclosure, theirs was a considerable innovation; 'Your convent', said Vincent de Paul, 'will be the house of the sick; your cell a hired room; your chapel, a parish church; your cloister, the streets of the city or the wards of the hospital; your enclosure, obedience; your grill, the fear of God; your veil, holy modesty.'

Secondly, must be noticed the patience and care lavished on the undertaking, the training of the first sisters, preceded by the careful 'grooming' of Louise de Marillac herself at Vincent's hands. The work grew and prospered because it was built on solid foundations; risks were taken, of course, on occasion, in the carrying out of this or that charitable work that was urgently necessary, but they were calculated risks, run with the knowledge that heavenly help would be forthcoming in a work that was primarily for the glory of God and the good of others.

Lastly, and principally, what is especially noteworthy in this biography is the careful delineation of the growth in holiness of a woman who started her life under some disadvantages and who, we should say nowadays, probably suffered in her early years from the unresolved complexes caused by her disturbed childhood and adolescence. By the time that she came under the firm direction of Vincent de Paul she was beginning to find the way to the resolution of her psychological difficulties and he was able to guide her surely and patiently into calm waters, but the scars remained for a long time, perhaps even to the end, and it is the merit

of Mgr Calvet's study that he in no way diminishes this side
of the story.

It would be an exaggeration perhaps to say that the
portrait is painted 'warts and all', but the human element
is made sufficiently plain for us to discern wherein lay the
heroism of the holiness that is so clearly depicted. The
interrelation of body and soul, nature and grace, religion
and daily life, are important factors in any biography; in the
biography of a saint they would seem to be paramount,
because unless proper account is taken of them we are
presented with one of the stock figures which appear to have
no connection with the world in which they lived and worked;
we fail to see what made them what they were, what caused
them to be saints. In reading Mgr Calvet's account of
Louise de Marillac we are left in no doubt about this: the
woman and saint both appear very clearly and we are able
to discern without difficulty what may be called the con-
stituents of her sanctity. And in Vincent's relations with her
and the fascinating correspondence that passed between
them, we catch a glimpse of the workings of grace in two
souls; Vincent frequently the vehicle of grace for Louise,
helping her, advising her and protecting her from the pitfalls
of her temperament, restraining the impatience that she
sometimes showed to go forward too rapidly, and calming
her ever-recurring fears. But if Vincent helped Louise, there
can be no doubt either that Louise helped Vincent on his
own way heavenwards. The interplay of character and mind
between two persons, particularly when they are bound, as
were Vincent and Louise, by the bonds of affection and
duty, is never all in one direction, and Louise's contribution,
though less obvious, was considerable. She appears in these
pages as a woman whose holiness was built on the trials and
tribulations of a life of no ordinary circumstances, and who
became a saint by following God's call to minister to his poor.

PART I

THE MYSTERY OF HER ANCESTRY AND YOUTH

MARILLAC FAMILY ORIGINS

IT IS HARD today to appreciate the role played by the great families of France in the seventeenth century; they stood between the nobility on the one hand, and the rising bourgeoisie on the other, a group of powerful old families, holding in their hands the effective *administrative* power of the country. They formed the lesser nobility and the judicial class, the *noblesse de robe*, many of them holding large estates by right of inheritance. They were the members of the *parlements*, the holders of the key military posts, of the bishoprics, the abbeys, the embassies, the titles and offices of the magistrature, and positions in the central government.

In 1590, when Louise de Marillac was born, these families were still the real strength of the nation, the active and influential core of French society. The Marillacs were long-standing and important members of this class. They came originally from the region of Mauriac, in Le Cantal, that cold and rugged part of Auvergne which is as hard as the rock of its river beds. In the thirteenth century they were already making themselves felt. A fifteenth-century head of the house, Guillaume de Marillac, definitely brought the family to the front ranks. Two of his children acquired fame. Charles, a diplomat, was ambassador at Constantinople, in London, and in the Low Countries, and later Archbishop of Vienna. Guillaume, who was always known as 'Guillaume II', to distinguish him from his father, became eminent as a financer. By 1569 he had risen to be controller general to the king.

This 'Guillaume II' married twice, in 1560 and 1571. By his first wife, Renée Alligret, he had eight children, among them Louis de Marillac, seigneur de Ferrières, the father of our Louise, and Michel who rose to be Keeper of the Seals and eventually Chancellor of France, the first gentleman of the realm after the King. By his second wife, Geneviève de Bois-Lévéque, Guillaume had four sons. One of these, Louis, comte de Beaumont, entered the army and eventually became marshal of France. A daughter by this second marriage, Valence, married Doni d'Attichy, Superintendent of Finances to Queen Marie de' Medici.*

In this torrent of great names, we tend to overlook Louis, lord of Ferrières and Farinvilliers, eldest son of Guillaume II. He was to some extent eclipsed by his brothers, and quite outdistanced by the brilliant marriage of his half-sister. Yet he was as handsome as any of them and had as good a head, though something of a fop and ladies' man. By profession he was a soldier, a captain of the guard in the royal household. He died young, at forty-eight years of age, leaving no mark on history save that he was the father of Louise.

Thus Louise de Marillac was born of a sturdy line, and came from a family of high ambition which was nourished by the noblest of alliances and the finest of natural gifts and graces. She was destined to play a far-reaching role in the religious and social history of her country, and to achieve happiness for herself. But in her youth, and for long after, she was bowed down by the weight of a mysterious dispensation of providence.

* See Appendix for fuller details of the careers of these members of the Marillac family.

THE MYSTERY OF HER BIRTH

THE FACTS are as follows: Louis de Marillac, lord of Ferriéres en Brie and later also of Farinvilliers, spent his youth in the army and carried out with competence the commissions with which he was entrusted. In 1584, he married Marie de la Rozière, a kinswoman of his father's first wife. In 1588 or '89 she died, childless.

Louise was born on 12th August, 1591. If we had her certificate of baptism, we should probably know her mother's name. But the registers for the years 1590 to 1595 have disappeared from the archives.

To fill this blank, historians have suggested a marriage between Louis and one Marguerite Le Camus in 1590. But of this lady and this marriage no trace can be found. If this Marguerite had existed, the genealogists, always so pain-staking, would surely have made some reference to her. As things stand and until the contrary be proved, we must say that Louise was born of Louis de Marillac and an unknown mother. From the day of her birth, her father provided for her by settling on her an annual pension of 100 livres, and by the bequest of a field on the Ferrières domain.

On January 12th, 1595, Louis de Marillac contracted a second marriage, with Antoinette Le Camus, aunt of Jean-Pierre Camus, who was later Bishop of Belley, and friend of Francis de Sales. Ten days before the date of the contract, Louis made further provision for his daughter:

'Before the undersigned, Toussaint Gleaume and Claude Trouvé, notaries of our lord the King, in Le Châtelet at Paris, there appeared in person Louis de Marillac, knight, resident at Paris in the rue St Antoine in the parish of St Paul, who recognises and acknowledges, and by these presents acknowledges to have given . . . to

Louise de Marillac, his natural daughter, being absent
... eighty-three and one-third *écus* in payment of an annual
and perpetual pension. . . . The said . . . renunciations
being made for the good friendship which he has always
had, and has, for the said testatrix, and so that she shall
have the better means to support herself after the death
of the said testator, and to provide for her marriage. . . .'

Louis settled on her after his death an annual pension of
83 *écus*, or 235 *livres*, payable quarterly.

It is remarkable that in this official document Louis de
Marillac should describe Louise as 'ma fille, ma naturelle'—
his 'natural daughter'. He knew that she was legally incapable
of inheriting from her father, even though recognised by him,
and that this was a principle on which Church law agreed
with civil law. The contract for his second marriage, which
took place shortly after the date of this settlement and which
enumerates the qualifications of the bridegroom, makes no
mention at all of his daughter Louise, as if she did not, in
law, exist. On the other hand, specific mention is made that
Antoinette Le Camus, the widow Thiboust, had four children,
who are all named, and who were at that date being sup-
ported by the public funds.

On December 28th, 1601, there was born of this marriage
a daughter, Innocente. Since she was legitimate, this child
was fully capable in law of inheriting property and possessions
from her father. Once again Louis de Marillac settled upon
Louise, his natural daughter, a sum of money, 1,200 *livres*,
and a small personalty (which, in those days, meant such
things as linen and jewels). It looks as though he was taking
a further step for the protection of his first child.

Finally, in the marriage contract of Louise herself with
Antoine Le Gras, in 1613, Louise being present and signing,
she is described as the natural daughter of the late Louis de
Marillac, and there is no mention of the name of her mother.

In the present state of our knowledge of the de Marillac
family, it is evident that Louise was born out of wedlock, that

she was illegitimate in law, that she was recognised by her father and that her mother was a person of such condition that, by the social customs of his class, Louis de Marillac could neither marry nor recognise her. It is very probable that she was a servant-girl. Society drew a great distinction between the child of an unknown father, especially if abandoned by the mother, and the child born out of wedlock of an unknown mother and a father who recognised and reared it. The first was a foundling and would always live on the fringes of society. The second was 'the son of his father', recognised as such, and deprived only of legal claims upon the family. The Church herself (in the question of admission to holy orders) drew a distinction between the two classes of illegitimacy. When, in our own day, the question arose of introducing the cause of Louise de Marillac, the Superior-General of the Mission and of the Daughters of Charity enquired in Rome whether her birth would not be an obstacle to her beatification. The reply was negative and the cause was therefore provisionally introduced.

Why have we stressed these details which earlier writers on Louise have, as though by common consent, appeared not to know, or passed over in silence, or concealed? We believe the facts are important for the better understanding of her mind, of the pattern of her life, and of the special ways in which her activities developed. A nature such as hers, where everything discloses a sensitivity without protection, and the sorrowful forcefulness of intuition, must have been shaken to its depths on that day—and it occurred at an early age—when the child first learned the facts of her origin.

We will not speak of revolt, for that would be out of character and would introduce an element of romance out of keeping with our subject. The nobles of France were accustomed to disregard sentimental considerations and the conventions; I would be inclined to say morality also, were it not that, in recognising the fault, they did acknowledge the existence of a fundamental morality. Louise did not 'rebel' but she was bent and bowed down by a burden mysteriously laid upon her in her cradle.

We know nothing of her infancy. Her father appears to have loved her dearly and to have taken all the care of her that his frequent changes of domicile allowed. He declares in his will, with transparent truthfulness, that Louise had been given him to be his consolation in affliction.

After her father's remarriage, in 1895, how did Louise get on in the care of Antoinette Le Camus, with her family of three daughters and one son, already quite grown up? It is useless to berate the stepmother. She may have been affectionate towards Louise. But the latter never, to our knowledge, spoke of her. And we do know certain things about Antoinette which give us cause to think. We learn that in 1602, after the birth of Innocente, Louis, returning from Lyons, brought a court action against his wife, Antoinette, for some kind of misconduct into which 'she had been driven by urgent need of money'. There is evidence of a double interrogation of the accused woman, of an indictment, and even of a confrontation of accuser and accused in court. What could have been the occasion for such a process in law—since, in the old French legal system, divorce was not recognised—we do not know. Perhaps it was to obtain an injunction against the squandering of the family funds. At all events, it is evident that the domestic atmosphere was disturbed and scarcely favourable to the upbringing and happiness of a ten-year-old girl.

In fact, Louise was no longer at home. We do not know the exact date that her father, as a matter of prudence and to give her a distinguished education, placed Louise in the royal convent at Poissy. This was a house of Dominican nuns, and its prioress was a Gondi—a member of one of those great families of Italian origin which, as we have mentioned, controlled in this period every sphere of French public life. Under her rule the life of the house was tranquil and fervent, though still untouched by the reforms which had become widespread in religious houses since the Council of Trent. To this fashionable convent came the children of the most eminent families; it was said—with what truth we cannot tell —to bestow a classical education.

At least there was in this community—and perhaps she was not exceptional—a humanist nun of some eminence in her day: Louise de Marillac, great-aunt of our Louise. She had a reputation for piety and wisdom, was a lover of the fine arts and had a knowledge of both Latin and Greek. She had rendered the 'Little Office of Our Lady' into very elegant French. She was naturally put in charge of the little girl's education and took a delight in teaching her, finding in her exceptional gifts. It is not without significance that the future saint should at an early age, and for some years, have been in close association with a fine mind of this stamp. She was saved, once for all, from futility and acquired a taste for intellectual food of a very solid kind. More than one bio- grapher has testified, for example, to the range of her knowledge of philosophy, a subject on which she is said to have conducted long conversations with her father.* She developed a taste for painting in oils, an art in which she became an adept: she acquired a good knowledge of Latin as then taught, for the reading of classical authors and as an accomplishment. Vincent de Paul put a somewhat dry emphasis on this ability of hers, when with the faintest touch of malice he happened to quote in a letter some Latin passage or other: 'You will be sure to understand this Latin, so I won't translate it'. 'This Latin' became part of the architecture of her mind. It gave her language a robust precision, her spirituality the sap of the liturgy and of theology, and perhaps her heart the joy of a more direct contact with a Church which prays in the language of St Jerome and thus enabled her to conform ever more closely with the tradition of Rome.

(*) There may be some slight exaggeration here, since when her father died in 1604, Louise was no more than thirteen years of age. (*Author.*)

Everything leads us to believe that the period spent at
Poissy was entirely happy, far from the storms of her father's
home, in the innocence and carefreeness of youth, in the
society of an aunt who knew so many things and in an
environment which could not but gratify the daughter of a
great house.

THE MYSTERY OF THE 'POOR DEMOISELLE'

THEN LOUISE was withdrawn from the convent school at Poissy. When? Why? On whose authority? Of all those strange mysteries which abound in the childhood story of Louise de Marillac, this is the most obscure.

Was she taken away by her father in 1602, when his law-suit with Antoinette de Camus was stretching his resources? Or did she have to leave after his death in 1604, because no one else would come forward to pay her fees, which must have been high? Most of her biographers have recorded that she was removed 'so that she could be taught those things which a woman ought to know', meaning, we may suppose, the crafts of housekeeping, cooking and dressmaking. Were such things, then, not taught by the learned ladies of Poissy? It is difficult to understand such anxiety, to the extent of taking her away from her studies at the age of thirteen, for the domestic formation of a child of noble family, whose grandfather had controlled the finances of a queen.

Who could have intervened in such a way? Who acted as her tutor? Other biographers have naturally considered the grave and forceful Michel de Marillac, her uncle, and master of pleas in the *Parlement*. It is known that Michel was at one time tutor to her half-sister, Innocente, but we have no knowledge that he had anything to do with the education of Louise.

It looks as if, her father being dead, Louise was abandoned with indifference by the entire family. They turned their back upon this child who had no rightful place in the genealogical tree, this girl who, most embarrassingly, bore the Marillac name and who must therefore be found a home somewhere or other. Louise was now thirteen years old; she knew and understood; and her heart was wounded. Her vocation to suffering was being made plain to her.

There could be no question of Louise returning to her father's home to live with Antoinette Le Camus; she made not the slightest overture to her step-daughter. Louise had her small pension, her few personal possessions, her little nest-egg; these would suffice to maintain her in some modest lodging. So it came about that she was boarded with a 'poor spinster', a woman who had already gathered around her a number of destitute children of about the same age as Louise. At a later day, such a home would have been called a 'dame school', or even a 'domestic school', and here Louise was to begin to learn 'those things which a woman ought to know', and which most small children learn at their mother's knee.

The 'poor spinster' seems in this way to have gained a living of sorts. Her house was apparently literally an orphanage, and she had a struggle to make ends meet. Louise, a girl of warm feeling, with already plenty of decision and a practical mind, speedily devised means to help. She persuaded Mademoiselle to allow into the house the materials for all sorts of domestic work. She rallied the other girls to her help, with such good results that 'Mademoiselle' began to find herself well provided for by the income from the lace, embroidery and linen goods made by her pupils and other guests. There was no lack of work; we know the importance of embroideries and laces in the fashions of the time, not least in male attire.

We cannot but admire the spirit of this child, who emerges from the shelter of a royal convent and proceeds, with all the simplicity of a peasant girl, to bring well-being to a woman who is a stranger to her. That holiness which had already struck roots in her soul was moving her to great achievements. We are full of admiration for her, but it is difficult to understand the terrible silence, the frozen indifference of her noble family, who could abandon to the hard life of a working girl an orphan child of their own blood. Nor is it any easier to sympathise with 'Mademoiselle', who was content to live on the labour of her boarder. There must be an explanation for these curious circumstances, and there is no reason why we should not risk an hypothesis, and see whether it leads to a solution of the mystery. We will argue as follows:

We do not at present know who was the mother of Louise. Yet a mother she certainly had, and apparently the woman came from the peasant class, since the Marillac family would not acknowledge her. She may have been a domestic servant, but she was in any case one whom, by the usages of his day and class, the child's father could not marry. The man is none the less a Christian; he has his principles. He will not suppress the woman, and neither can he just turn her out and so sentence her to a life of wretchedness. Is it not possible that he looked around him for some means which would enable her to earn a living—even that he set her up in a boarding house for orphan girls, the children of unknown mothers? And having so established her, why not entrust to her care their own daughter, at a time when his shrinking means made it impossible to keep her at the royal convent at Poissy?

Even if such a plan did not occur to Louis himself, yet his brothers, to whom every detail of the child's circumstances must have been known, could well make provision of this kind when the father died, which would dispense them from the more human and natural act of taking the orphan girl into one of their own families. By such an arrangement, every responsibility would have been discharged: the mother was succoured without being acknowledged; the child was in a place of safety; ihey would be able to develop affection for each other with no harm done to public opinion. Justice, morality, sensibility were satisfied, and all concerned could sleep quietly. Louise would thus have spent the years of her adolescence (1604-1613) in the company of her own mother, who tenderly loved her, and who taught her the domestic arts—with what success, we shall see presently.

It is true that this hypothesis does not at present rest upon any documentary evidence. But there is nothing impossible about it and it is reassuring. The silence of a large, powerful and wealthy family creates around the orphan girl a lamentable desert. If we adopt this theory, the desert disappears. Those who keep silence know that they may do so without injustice; and the orphan is no longer alone.

We have the impression that Louise was well advised and guided in the defence of her interests. As the law stood, it was her half-sister, Innocente, who inherited the lands and personal property of their father, and who was bound to pay Louise the rents and pensions provided by contract. There is evidence that these monies were not regularly paid, for two judgments, recorded at Le Chatelet, order her tutor—who is none other than her uncle, Michel de Marillac—to pay to Louise, in the name of Innocente, a pension of 300 *livres* per annum. This is the clearest evidence we have as to her means, and it is the obvious source of the dowry of which she made conveyance at the time of her marriage in 1613.

We have a certain amount of light upon her spiritual development between 1604 and 1613, from her thirteenth to her twenty-second year. The 'poor spinster' was not of the calibre of Soeur Marillac at Poissy, but she could assure that stability in which the early lessons could sink in and take root. Even without the constant help of tutors and masters, a proud intelligence which begins to feel the driving force of its own gifts will find the elements of culture in all things. Louise devoted herself seriously to painting, her favourite art, and it is probably from this period that we should date her water-colours, so touching in their simplicity. Her subjects are religious, for such was the natural tendency of her soul; she had been brought up in habits of piety, and breathed an atmosphere that was entirely Christian. We would give much to know what were the books she read in these years to have acquired the spiritual culture so plainly revealed in her letters and notebooks. She herself mentions Luis of Granada, the

Spanish theologian and moralist, whose *Guide for Sinners* achieved a success which has endured to our own day. Vincent de Paul valued this book highly, and constantly returned to it. Luis is master of a form of stern and practical meditation which is always confronting the Christian with his own conscience, compelling him to exhaustive self-examination, and imposing resolutions wisely made but hard to keep. He does indeed preach love, but his love is not a gentle passion. The *Imitation of Christ* is quite different—it invites with sweetness, teaching the very elements of love. We know from her own statements that Louise de Marillac read both these books. It is probable, although she does not mention it, that she also read *The Pearl of the Gospels* (*La Perle Evangélique*) by the Flemish nun, a book which had lately been translated by Dom Beaucousin, and which was then in vogue with the devout laity. Later on, when she had obtained the necessary authorisation, she read the whole of the Scriptures. She heard the Jesuit and Capuchin preachers, reflected and meditated. In after years she confided in Marguerite Chetif, and told her that from her childhood she had had the attraction to meditation, and that it came to her easily. She spent much of her time in religious houses, which were then attracting the faithful by the renewed vigour of their observance and by their fervour.

These years at the beginning of the seventeenth century were for the Church, and especially for the devout laity, a time of spiritual renewal and opportunity. The long agony of the Wars of Religion had drawn to a close and the Church was recuperating after the struggle. The wise administration of Henri IV was creating in the civil sphere the material framework for a religious revival, while the spiritual incentives and the necessary ecclesiastical discipline had been provided by the Council of Trent. The Council's measures had received widespread assent as salutary and necessary, even before their formal promulgation, so that for the Church the present was full of activity, and the future full of promise.

A young girl who was both pious and cultivated could not remain indifferent to the many manifestations of new spiritual life which she was able to see on every hand, especially when she had strong private reasons, and family reasons too, for noticing these developments in the religious life of France.

The Jesuits returned in 1603, and inaugurated a form of preaching entirely free from political bias. The Carmelite nuns of St Teresa of Avila were installed in Paris in 1605: their arrival and installation in Paris were the occasion of ceremonies and processions in which all the devout and the high-born of Paris took active part. Michel de Marillac was one of those who met the Spanish nuns at Longjumeaux, and headed the joyful procession into Paris. It was he who handed them the keys of their new house in the name of Queen Marie de' Medici and of the Duchesse de Longueville, taking so zealous a part in the proceedings that Madame Acarie (whose mission it had been to inspire the work from behind the scenes) told him he was temporal founder of Carmel and Bérulle its spiritual father in France.

In 1606, the Duchesse de Mercoeur, carrying out a wish of the widow of King Henri III, established the Capuchin nuns in Paris. The nuns entered Paris in procession, barefooted, the Archbishop of Paris in person at their head. The nuns set a striking example of the strictest asceticism, and radiated the light of Franciscan devotion. Well-known Capuchin friars befriended and assisted them: Father Joseph, the renowned 'Grey Eminence', confessor to Richelieu; Father Benet Canfield; and Father Honoré de Champigny. The last-named friar was a relative of Madame Barbe Acarie and a connection of Michel de Marillac. He was for a while confessor or director to Louise.

In 1608, there appeared the *Introduction to the Devout Life* by Francis de Sales. Francis de Sales was a close friend of Madame Acarie and Michel de Marillac, and he had left behind him in Paris a memory of sweetness and light. Louise had read the *Introduction*, and we know how greatly she loved it. It is probable that she also read the *Sainte Philosophie* of Du Vair, and the *Bref Discours* which, if not actually written by Bérulle, contains the essence of his teaching, in which Louise was steeped. So we can trace the foundation of her spiritual attitudes and see the growth of her habitual approach, the blend of contemplation and action, the union of love and reason.

There remain many features of this period of her life which are most obscure, and one which is very perplexing. This is the question of her dealings with her uncle, Michel de Marillac. We encounter this man at the opening out of every new path in the life of his niece—yet we never meet them together. At a later date he wrote her a number of letters, which we possess, but it does not appear that he ever took any very direct interest in her affairs. He was a man of prayer, and three times a week he discoursed with Madame Acarie on the way of perfection. He could have had an important influence on the spiritual formation of Louise, a girl of exceptional gifts. Yet there is nothing to indicate that he ever made the attempt. It is difficult to avoid the impression that to some extent he shared the embarrassment of the family and cared but little for a girl who could not be disavowed, yet who could not be given a position in the family tree.

The family kept clear of her and this caused the child much suffering. The world rejected her—yet God drew her to himself. It is easy to understand that she should have wished to become a nun, and to shut herself up in their convent with the Capuchin sisters, devoted to a life of penance and prayer. This would have solved all the problems that perplexed her mind, and soothed away the troubles of her soul. She discussed the matter with her confessor, Father Honoré de Champigny, and he must have discussed the subject with his friend, Michel de Marillac.

Louise had a weak constitution. Her life was already what it would always be, an uninterrupted sequence of mild illnesses, no single one of which could ever put her life in danger, but which made it necessary for her to exercise constant care of her health. The Rule of St Clare, rigid and unyielding, would certainly not suit her, nor the Rule of our Holy Mother, St Teresa. Father de Champigny declared to her, as from God, that she could not become a nun, but that it was his belief 'that God had some other design for her'. What a disappointment—a setback the more serious because it came too late. She had already taken the first steps, and secretly committed herself by promise to become a nun. It is said, and Louise herself said, that she made no vow. It does not appear that there was ever any question of a formal vow creating an obligation in conscience, either with or without her director's consent and advice. But years afterwards, in a time of anxiety, she came to believe that she had committed herself, and that by her marriage she had broken her vow. This was the dramatic crisis which opened the greatest trial of her life. The dramas of the life of the soul, though they are very often mere banks of cloud, will sometimes precipitate the most devastating tempests.

She could not, then, become a nun; there was no other course open to her but marriage. In later life, she insisted that she had a true vocation to the cloister, and that she only married out of obedience to her 'relatives'. Who were the relatives who would urge her to marry? Certainly not Michel, who had considered her welfare but little, and not Louis, who was absent on military service. Valence was a woman of generosity, and she would well understand Louise's anxieties, and it may have been she who counselled her to find a husband.

It would be possible, if not exactly easy, to find her a husband. Like all her family, she was handsome. The portrait that we have of her is based on a painting by Dechange, made from memory after her death. It is therefore separated by time from the model, but tradition declares it to be a faithful likeness. It depicts a face which is very regular, within the lines of a perfect oval. The veil, covering her head and part of her face, casts over her features a shadow which the artist has preserved, but which tends to make her look plain, though we are informed that her expression was one of vivacious originality. The mouth is small, the lips thin, the chin prominent and firm. The eyes, lowered as is fitting in a nun, shine, as we may suppose, with a restrained fire. She so often spoke to her Daughters of Charity of the eyes, and of the manner of using them; of the obligation to mortify them out of doors, yet without closing them; of the fruitful meditation that may be made on the eyes of Jesus, which, as the Gospels tell us, were subject to his will—that we may well believe her own eyes to have been beautiful, clear, luminous, the mirror of an impassioned soul. Yes, we may say that she was beautiful.

Louise may be described as handsome, but she was not wealthy. The whole of her fortune was the little pension of 300 *livres* which had been guaranteed to her by the Chatelet judgment. The few personal possessions given her by her father in 1602 she had left behind with Mademoiselle. She had little enough by way of dowry, but to compensate for the lack of means, she had relatives who were in a fair way to make large fortunes: an uncle and an aunt of the Queen Mother; a master of pleas in the *parlement* bestowed by the queen on Richelieu; and the queen's superintendent of finances. Finally, whether the family liked it or not, she was a Marillac, and the name was a most valuable asset.

A GREAT MARRIAGE OF CONVENIENCE

For Valence de Marillac and Catherine de' Medici, wife of Louis de Marillac, it was no very difficult matter to find somewhere about the Court a young man with a future, who would make a suitable husband for Louise. Choice was made of Antoine Le Gras, Secretary of the Household to the Queen, Marie de' Medici, a sufficiently minor official, but with a future more than promising. He was a mere squire, and not a gentleman, so that his wife would not be entitled to the style of 'Madame', but only to that of 'Mademoiselle', like any other woman of the bourgeoisie. The family was originally of Montferrand in Auvergne, where the surname in use was 'Gras'. But when they rose in the social scale and settled in Paris, they inserted an article before the surname, which made them upper middleclass and on the way to rank, as members of the *noblesse de robe*. They were of old and honourable stock, steady and regular in business, especially good and charitable to the poor. Moreover, they combined with a very orderly administration of inherited property a most persevering attention to their further enrichment. Little is recorded of Antoine Le Gras beyond his health, which was poor, and his temper, which was quick. He appears to have been rather dull, better fitted to attend to small matters, albeit with dexterity, than to embark on great ones.

The marriage contract was drawn up and signed at the Hotel d'Attichy, residence of the Superintendent of Finances to the Queen Mother. It was thought appropriate on this auspicious occasion to accredit the bride with a domicile above reproach: she was stated in the document to be a resident in the Hotel d'Attichy. The marriage bond was witnessed by a series of very honourable names.

'There were present in person, M. Antoine Le Gras,

secretary to the Queen mother of the King, son of the late noble gentleman, M. Antoine Le Gras, in his lifetime a Councillor, and elected for the King in the election of Clermont in Auvergne, and of Damoiselle Marguerite, *née* Atour, his wife; these his father and mother being likewise present, being resident at this time in Paris, rue des Francbourgeois in the parish of Saint-Gervais, to speak for him and in his name; on the one hand; and Damoiselle Loyse de Marillac, natural daughter of the late Louis de Marillac, in his lifetime Knight, lord of Farinvilliers, using and having the enjoyment of her rights, and living in the residence of the Sieur and Dame d'Attichy hereinafter named, to speak for her and in her name; on the other hand;

The which parties of their goodwill recognised and acknowledged as lawful the future marriage which in the good pleasure of God is shortly to be made and solemnised in the face of holy Church between these two, in the presence and by the advice of Messire Octavien Dony d'Attichy, counsellor to the King in Council, Intendant of his finances and of those of the household of the Queen; Dame Valence de Marillac, his wife; Messire Michel de Marillac, counsellor to the King in Council; Louis de Marillac, gentleman in ordinary of the bed-chamber to the King; Dame Catherine de' Medici, his wife; Damoiselle Cornelia Dony, widow of the late Sieur Goriny; Dame Genevieve Dony, wife of Sieur le comte de Chateauvillain; Messire Paul de Miremont, lord of Montigny; Dame Victoire Scolary, his wife; and Damoiselle Louyse Hennequin, widow of the Sieur de Vernoy, counsellor in the Court of Pleas at the Palais; all being mutual friends of the two betrothed parties aforesaid.'

Even if we assume that Louise was already advanced in humility, she was too much a woman not to regard this brilliant gathering as some compensation for the bitterness of

her years as a poor pensioner. True, there was still bitterness
mingled with the sweet. She had to hear read, and she had to
sign, a document which particularised the ancestry of her
future husband, and named his father and mother, while it
described Louise herself in blunt terms as 'the natural
daughter of Louis de Marillac', and made no mention of her
mother's name. Those eminent persons, moreover, who added
their signatures as witnesses to the foot of the contract—
Michel and Louis, her uncles, Valence and Catherine, her
aunts—were merely styled as 'friends'. An iron law regulated
even such trifles as these, and played its part at every stage
of the proceedings.

After the religious ceremony in the church of Saint-
Gervais these particular clouds were dissipated: there was
no longer any need to look for a place for Louise in the de
Marillac family tree. Before God and in full view of society
she was Mademoiselle Le Gras, attached by marriage to the
household of the Queen Mother. The young couple was
borne up on a wave of hope and public favour. She now had
her hour of well-being; upon her were fixed the eyes of many
who hoped for recommendations and support in their
approach to the great. She was ready to take her rightful
place in public life, for we hear of the Le Gras family
incurring, in their palace in the Marais, heavy expenses for
household maintenance and for entertainment. The bill
amounted to more than 18,000 *livres* per annum. They also
added a turret to the building. This turret, which made no
pretensions to being a tower, marked a stage on the family's
journey towards the nobility. The palace was kept in
fashionable style and attracted that youthful and vivacious
section of Parisian society which was then turning to account
the rapid rise to fortune of the Concini. Louise had met both
Concini, the Marechal d'Ancre, and his wife Leonora at the
home of Michel de Marillac, at which, as she tells us herself,
she was now a frequent visitor, and at the home of Louis,
always absent himself, where Catherine de' Medici, his wife,

virtuous and radiant, shed light on all around her. Mademoiselle Le Gras could almost meet high society at the Hôtel Doni d'Attichy, where the children were most attached to her. Anne, in particular, who grew up to become the comtesse de Maure, loved her dearly. She was also frequently to be seen about the Court of Henri IV, to which her duty, if not her taste, bound her firmly.

This period of happiness, and even of brilliant social success, a time made brighter still by the birth of her son, Michel, on 19th October, 1613, was not of long duration. A brief and devastating storm wrecked many an illusion. Concini, the Marechal d'Ancre, was assassinated; the queen was disgraced and exiled to Blois and it is not certain whether her secretary, Le Gras, followed her into retirement, or remained with his wife in Paris. The vivid group of social climbers which had grouped itself about the Medici was scattered and stunned. Earthly fortunes change and no human disposition is secure.

Louise suffered keenly throughout these months of political crisis and she was also assailed by anxieties of a more personal nature. She loved her child with a warm and tremulous passion, but the boy was dull-witted, and only very slowly did his mind develop. This son, as we shall see, was to be a constant trial to her and a cross to be carried to the very end of her life. Now she was racked with anxiety, straining all her powers to emancipate that backward mind from the thraldom of an ungainly body.

The Doni d'Attichy died, in the flower of his youth. That was in 1615, and Valence followed him in 1619. They left behind them seven children and a seriously embarrassed estate. Michel de Marillac, the children's tutor, burdened with a thousand other cares, invited Antoine Le Gras to take over the management of the d'Attichy property. Antoine had met his wife in the d'Attichy household and had not forgotten the delicate courtesies of Valence and her husband: he readily undertook the duty. With much patience and by

B

skilful management he was able to save the children from imminent ruin, but he was of a generosity so immoderate that in preventing their beggary he incurred a certain risk of precipitating his own. He neglected his business, pledged his property, and parted with a great deal of his capital. These are the terms that Louise uses, complaining gently of her husband's conduct, though she was undoubtedly just as warmly concerned as he was. Love can be a tyrant, and gratitude sometimes becomes an imposition. It came to pass that the d'Attichy children took offence at the assiduous services of Antoine Le Gras, and gave Louise to understand that they could recall a time when she herself had stood in need of succour. The wound thus wilfully inflicted must have been a sharp one, for Michel de Marillac, a man of known discretion, was obliged to intervene. He had to rebuke his d'Attichy nephews for their lack of manners, and reminded Louise of the virtue of forbearance.

In all these ways, bitter sufferings worked on Louise's soul and penetrated it, and they found her fully open to their attack. Throughout her youth her soul had been cramped in the exercise of its powers, and now she could do no more than resign herself to sorrow, as to a fate laid on her in her cradle.

SHE PASSES THROUGH A CRISIS OF DEPRESSION

LOUISE was not plunged into this state of confusion and weakness all at once. She resisted temptations. She profited from her trials, striving to ground herself in humility and the thought of her own nothingness, seeking in reading and meditation a firm spiritual foundation for her life. Though we do not know in detail what they were, we are told that she had a considerable collection of books. She asked permission for herself and her husband to read the Bible in its unabridged form—a freedom which was in those days a privilege for the laity. She had also the joy of reading the *Treatise of the Love of God*, by St Francis de Sales, in all the freshness of its original text, in 1616. Her biographers affirm, without offering evidence, that she was acquainted with the author and that he visited her during one of her illnesses. This is very possible, in view of the close relations between Michel de Marillac and Francis de Sales. Whether or not Louise knew him personally, she had a warm admiration for him and a confident trust which amounted to veneration, as of a saint whom she had canonised for her own use.

We catch a glimpse of the habitual tendency of her thoughts from a few letters that we have, written to her at this time by Michel de Marillac. These letters are rather cool and detached, and as we read them we are astonished to find never a word of affection, never a word, nor any advice on some particular point or urgent matter. They allude occasionally to letters written by Louise to him, and apparently also to conversations. Michel preaches to her the Berullian doctrine of self-abnegation and humility in terms a little stilted, but undoubtedly earnest.

Mademoiselle,   Paris, 6th March, 1620
    ... For what remains, Mademoiselle, it is good to learn

from experience that God is not attached to our own plans and propositions, and that those souls find him everywhere who seek him according to the manner in which he wills to communicate himself, and not according to their own conception of the manner which would be useful and profitable to themselves, for very often such usefulness imagined by the mind is no more than the satisfaction of their own feelings. But the poor soul which knows itself to be such, and accepts that knowledge in peace, looks to God for whatever comes, without expecting his will to be done in this manner or in that. Such a soul is content to submit itself to God, and does not desire to prescribe to him in what manner he shall lead her. She accepts what comes, making use of all things with humility, gratitude and profit, remaining at all times poor in herself, content to do the best she can, without allowing herself to grieve for what she lacks, or for things that are not within her power. And to judge of a thing, whether or no it be within our power, we must put our trust in the experience gained from several attempts, and not in the promptings of our own inclination.

I pray that God may give you the grace to profit from this, and to advance every day in his fear and love.

Your very humble and affectionate servant,

DEMARILLAC.

Marillac is probably dealing here with scruples and anxieties with which Louise was beset and haunted; he probes the recesses of her conscience, and excites in her a sense of sin to which she was in any case only too liable. She stood more in need of encouragement than of humbling.

Paris, 12th August 1621

Mademoiselle,

The same principle which has for a long time now obsessed you in meditation about yourself causes your thoughts, in my opinion, to fall habitually into a state of dejection, because they are concerned with self-scrutiny, in the attempt to acquire the knowledge of self which will conduce to humility. It is not that I condemn these thoughts, which are good and useful, but they are not at times in season. It is always the same thing: too much preoccupation with one's formation of oneself; inability to bear this dereliction and privation of spirit; the inability, as you say, to arrive at self-abasement unless you go in your own way. Now, to want to attain self-abasement by one's own efforts is an act of power and capacity, and a soul entertaining such a desire cannot at the same time be regarding itself as poor: she is attempting to do a thing to which no one compels her, and a thing, moreover, which she must know she cannot do of herself. Now, to drive oneself into doing a thing presupposes that one believes oneself capable of doing it.

It is therefore more useful to the soul to recognise that it is still poor in the faculty of self-knowledge, and to set a proper value on itself: not at all to lament its own poverty, as you are doing, but, confessing itself to be poor, to ask of God true poverty of spirit, and to co-operate faithfully and with profit with the means God gives for acquiring it, such as: when we commit a fault, to draw from it a knowledge of those dispositions of the soul which have produced it; or, when we see good in another, we can acknowledge that we ourselves are less than he; in a word, the soul faithful to God has, at every moment, indications which will humble her, if only she is in a state of simplicity and poverty, knowing and acknowledging that she possesses nothing, and that she has not even a true knowledge of her own poverty! And being thus poor, she remains a beggar before God, who alone can do all things for her. He recalls her to knowledge, awakens her to the memory of all the good to be done, all the evil to be fled, and the more she strips herself of her own careful-ness and activity, the more clearly she will see what to

do, and what to leave undone. Let her business therefore
be with God! Let her seek, and let her love, Jesus Christ!
Let her bind herself to him! Let her honour his life, his
labours, and his sufferings. For all that remains, the
simple fidelity of the soul adhering to God, who lacks
nothing of which she can feel the need, or to which she
can return, will ensure that she is sufficiently supplied.

I commend myself to your good prayers, and am,
Mademoiselle, your very humble and affectionate servant,

DEMARILLAC.

Pierre Camus, Bishop of Belley, friend and disciple of
Francis de Sales, was more ready to help her. A nephew of
Antoinette, her father's second wife, he had met Louise and
treated her with affection and familiarity, calling her 'my
sister', or 'my daughter'; while Marillac was never more than
a spiritual adviser, Camus was a true director. To him also
Louise had confided those feelings which now so completely
dominated her: the obsession with the obscurity of her birth,
her consciousness of sin, her desire to renew her general
confession. He exhorts her to confidence and joy.

(1622?)

Mademoiselle, my dear sister,

Yours of 1st December only came into my hands on
15th January. I am answering it today, the 20th, as I had
no opportunity to do it earlier. I sympathise with you in
the inertia of mind in which you find yourself on account
of the illness of your dear husband. Come, then, here is
your cross, and why should I be sorry to see it on the
shoulder of a daughter of the Cross? To carry it well, you
do not lack skill, nor counsel, nor books, nor mind. God
desires also that you should not lack the courage.

You are always wanting to run to a general confession
as the jubilee comes round. How many times have I said
to you: Enough of these general confessions, for your
heart! Ah, no! The jubilee, for us, does not come round

again for that purpose, but to give us occasion to rejoice in God our Saviour, and to say: *jubilemus Deo, salutari nostro*. Oh, may God bless the paternal heart of M. de St Sauveur. Greet him from me, my dear sister, and also the dear husband and the dear little son, for I belong without division to you all,

> your very humble servant,
>
> *signed:* J.-P., *ev. de Belley.*

20th January, at Belley.

Greet also Mme Menard, mother of a good daughter, and daughter of a good mother, for I know she denies she is a lady of rank.

Yet Camus, though a man of fine mind as well as a holy bishop, had perhaps not sufficient forcefulness to restrain this woman on the dangerous slope down which she was slipping in consequence of self-questioning, self-analysis and self-contempt.

The crisis was deadly. It was precipitated by the illness of Antoine Le Gras. What this illness was, we do not know, but it lasted a long time—four or five years—and its first effect was to make him very irritable, a difficult patient. It was a heavy cross for Louise, and slowly the thought suggested itself to her that it was intended as a penalty. She was being punished because she had broken her vow to become a Capuchin sister, and therefore—so faulty is the logic of temptation—she should leave her husband, the father of her child, so as to enter into the spirit of her vow. This thought tormented her. She applied for help to the Visitation nuns, who were dear to her for the sake of Francis de Sales. The Mother Superior, Catherine de Beaumont, knowing her agony of mind, wrote to console her, inviting her to accept this sorrow as coming from the hand of God.

Vive Jésus!

I sympathise greatly with your sorrow, my very dear daughter, but all the same, I have no fear, but rather the hope that the hand which has inflicted the wound will work the cure. O God! Be therefore very gentle and courageous, to support with patience what is given you with so great a love. Do you think that God would make you suffer for any other reason than that you might acquire merit? We must leave the 'why?' with him, for it is no part of our business to know it, but to be very submissive to his good pleasure. Be so then, my dear daughter, and pay less attention to what you yourself are feeling and suffering; but unite your will to that of our heavenly Father, that you may do and suffer whatever pleases him; then after that, do everything you can for the health of your dear husband, leaving the outcome to the good pleasure of God. No, I have no news at all of M. Vincent. I pray God that he will strengthen you, and aid you with his grace. Pray for me also, who am to go on a little journey for perhaps three weeks. À Dieu, my dear daughter. May God be the joy and repose of your heart. I am, in him, unchangeably yours. Amen.

Our community will pray especially for you and for all. This Saturday, at noon, pausing only to bid you goodnight.

What should have been pointed out to her by them all, was the absurd element in this spiritual grief of hers. To reason with her about her obssession was only to strengthen it. Her directors were no use to her. And as one aberration brought another in its train, she formed the opinion that she was too much attached to her director, and must leave him, to follow for the future her own unsupported judgment. The moment thus to deprive herself of all help was ill-chosen. She proceeded to devise a most singular method of coming to terms with her vow. If her husband should die, she would take a vow of perpetual widowhood! So here was another vow! Did Camus advise it, or did he acquiesce in it for the sake of peace? There is little to admire in it. Assuredly, it is evidence of a great love of the religious life, and of a high degree of detachment. But a right-minded Christian woman

who is married, and whose husband is lying ill in the neigh-
bouring room, does not dream of taking a vow of widowhood; she pushes open the door, and goes in to nurse her
husband, so as to keep him alive. To make plans in view of
his death is merely repulsive.

A ridiculous remedy will not cure a stubborn complaint,
a disorder caused by a series of preposterous deductions.
Louise was whirled about like a bird tossing helplessly in a
storm. She fell from the sky and entered the night. She has
described it herself in a few colourless words. I quote from
the manuscript the complete text of her account, as other
biographers have given it in fragments only.

Feast of St Monica (May 4) 1623.

God gave me the grace to make a vow of widowhood,
if he should call away my husband. On Ascension Day
following, I fell into a great depression of mind which
lasted until Pentecost, because of the doubt which I had,
whether I ought to leave my husband, as I desire to do in
order to make atonement for my first vow, and to have
more liberty to serve God and my neighbour. I also
doubted whether the duty which I had to my director
was an impediment to my taking another, for I felt myself
obliged to leave him. I was also in great distress on
account of a doubt as to the immortality of the soul.

These three uncertainties gripped my soul with
torments such as, it seems to me, cannot be imagined.

Abandoned by God, she came to doubt herself, to doubt
the immortality of the soul and the very existence of God. She
passed the ten days between Ascension and Pentecost, 1623,
in a sort of opaque and desperate atheism. All the trials of
her childhood and youth were poured into this deadly
crucible, at the bottom of which she found nothing but
despair.

The violence of this earthquake need not astonish us. Such
crises are frequently met with in the lives of the saints and
persons of great spirituality, in the first stage of their ascent

towards perfection. At about this same time Vincent de Paul
was going through a similar trial, into which he had been
drawn by charity; he also came to doubt the existence of
God, to such an extent that his apostolic work was impeded.
Francis de Sales had known this trouble in his youth. Some
years later, Olier, another friend of M. Vincent, was to pass
through a long trial of the same kind, in the course of which
he seemed for long periods to be stupefied. Fénélon has put
on record the genuine mental depression he endured at the
time he entered into the mystic state.We may say that God
puts to the test those who engage themselves to serve him by
withdrawing from the crowd, and that he inflicts on them a
harsh and grievous psychological trial, which will become
one source of their fruitful activity.

From this pit of despair she called upon a God in whom,
so she imagined, she no longer believed. She also invoked the
assistance of Francis de Sales, who had but lately died (1622)
and who had once consoled her in a time of physical sickness.
All at once as in a dream, everything was changed: she felt a
great calm. Light flooded her—light bringing faith in God
and in Jesus Christ.

'On the feast of Pentecost I was in St Nicolas-des-
Champs during Holy Mass, and all in an instant my
mind was cleared of these doubts, and I was made to
realise that I must remain with my husband, and that a
time would come when I should be in a position to make
vows of poverty, chastity and obedience, and that this
would be done with persons where other women did the
same.

'I then understood myself to be in a place for the relief
and assistance of my neighbours, but I could not understand how this was being done, because these neighbours
were coming and going.

'I also understood that I was to be in peace as to my
director, and that God would give me one, whom he
caused me then to see, as I supposed, for I felt a repug-

nance about accepting him, but all the same I consented;
and it seemed to me that this was because I was not to
make this change just yet.

'My third burden was taken from me by the assurance
that I felt in my mind, that it was God who was teaching
me these things, and that since there was a God I ought
not to be doubtful about the other things. At that time,
the doubt as to immortality was leading me to disbelieve
in Divinity.

'I have always believed that I received this grace
through the blessed Monseigneur of Geneva, because I
had greatly desired, before his death, to communicate
these troubles to him, and since then I have felt towards
him a great devotion, and I have received through him
many gaces. At that time I had some matter about which
I sought his advice, but I cannot now remember what it
was. This happened on the feast of Pentecost, 1623, in the
church of St Nicolas-des-Champs, during the Mass.'

It was indeed the descent of the Holy Ghost. Louise de
Marillac was quite overwhelmed by the experience, of which
she retained a memory which became a part of her pro-
foundest being. She ever afterwards had a deep devotion to
the holy week between Ascension and Pentecost, and an
attentive and tender worship of the Holy Spirit.

From this time, she was troubled no more on the score of
her vows, but devoted herself to the care of her husband, who
was worn out by long suffering. She had the consolation of
seeing him become calmer, more resigned, and that her
presence beside him counted for something. There is a grace
for the sick in exercising charity towards them. Antoine Le
Gras died on 21st December, 1625. Her grief for him was
sincere. She has given expression to it, in words which cannot
disguise what she felt, in a letter to Pére Hilarion Rebours.

'Very Reverend Father,
    Since you wish to know what graces our good Lord

bestowed on my late husband, when I have said that it is impossible for me to make them all known, I will tell you that for a long time now, by the mercy of God, he no longer had any affection for those matters which can lead into mortal sin, and had a very great desire to live devoutly. Six weeks before his death he had a burning fever which put his mind in great danger, but God made apparent his power over nature, and restored calm. In gratitude for this grace, he resolved to serve God all his life. He scarcely slept at all at night; yet such was his patience that those who were with him were not in the least inconvenienced. I believe that in that last illness, God desired him to become a sharer in the pains of his own death; for he suffered in the whole of his body, and lost all his blood, while his mind was almost always occupied in meditation on the Passion. Seven times he lost blood from the mouth, the seventh time ending his life upon the instant. I was alone with him, to help him on this important journey, and he evidenced so much devotion, that he made us understand to his last breath this his mind was attached to God. He could never say more to me than: "Pray God for me, I can pray no more", words which are for ever engraved upon my heart. I beg you to remember him whenever you say Compline. He had so special a devotion to this Office, that he scarcely ever omitted to say it daily.'

Camus also gave her direction at intervals and now he wrote her, first the usual letter of consolation that every Christian heart expects, and then, since her reply showed that she had found no peace in her widowhood, he wrote her another letter of comfort. This second letter is singular, since it says in effect: 'You wanted to be a widow. You are a widow. What more do you want?'

My dear daughter, my dear sister,
The letter which I have received from you by the hands

of M. Chappe makes mention of two letters written by you. Of these, I have only seen one, which appears to have been written since the affliction of your widowhood. Now, my dear sister, I do not see why your mind is so troubled, and believes itself to be in shadows and abandonment. Why? You are no longer divided; now you belong wholly to the celestial Bridegroom, you have nothing now that is of the earth. You are resolved with all your mind to desire no other but him, and now you are astonished that he should have broken your bonds asunder and that you owe him a sacrifice of praise. O daughter of little faith, what do you fear? I must say to you what our Lord said to Mary on the resurrection of Lazarus. If you had more firmness of purpose, you would see the glory of God upon you. Yes, indeed! It is a thing I do not see clearly, but I know it for a certainty.

I am, Mademoiselle, your very humble servant.
26th March (1626)

The something more that Louise desired, and which Camus did not understand, was an escape from this universe in which she was stifling, and to be cured of her depression.

A SLOW CURE

BUT I have anticipated. When Camus wrote this consoling letter—which was a little beside the mark—he was no longer the actual director of Louise de Marillac. The director introduced by Providence in the vision in the church of St Nicolas-des-Champs had appeared on the scene. This was Vincent de Paul, and he had actually been put in touch with his penitent by Camus himself. Camus was now obliged to reside in his episcopal city of Belley—a sad place of exile, as he called it. Deprived of the two great Paris pulpits he had so much loved, he well knew that he would also have to give up spiritual direction. To take his place in the direction of Louise, he made choice of Monsieur Vincent, whom his friend, Francis de Sales, esteemed as a true man of God.

The first meeting of Vincent de Paul and Louise de Marillac was an event of incalculable significance. It brought about a revolution in the charitable activity of women, which from that time forth combined the life of perfection as lived by the cloistered nun with the life of activity in the world and literally, in the open air. This new form of charitable work took hold once and for all of the public spirit in France and thereafter throughout the world; it focused attention on the unfortunate and the sick, from which emerged the modern forms of social institution. One fact is indisputable. The world of today, where cruelty is so common in public conduct, dare not disdain the poor, and public men now make open profession of honouring the human dignity of the unfortunate and the weak. This is Christ's teaching put into action and is the result of Vincentian charitable works which are what they are because Louise de Marillac put her hand to them.

At first there were many difficulties to be overcome. Monsieur Vincent was reluctant to undertake spiritual direction which deflected him from his own vocation of the parochial mission. He knew from experience how burdensome could be the conscience of a woman of society. Madame de Gondi had done everything possible to persuade him that he ought to remain close to her to assist her in dying, which might occur at any moment, and she had said that he would be responsible for her damnation if she died alone and away from him. But he was reluctant to tie his hands in this way. Louise, for her part, did not feel drawn towards this rough, cold, worn-looking priest, a man far removed from the aristocratic polish and the radiant goodness of Camus and Francis de Sales. But both were very soon conscious of the need each had for the other, for a work as yet uncertain but which, as year followed year, would become more definite. Monsieur Vincent's devotion was entire and unwearied, as every moment and in every detail, for thirty-six years. At for Louise, her confidence in him was absolute, without shadow of doubt, and her submissive obedience to him knew no restriction. On both sides and in both hearts there was a clear-sighted affection, naïve in its intensity, the very ideal of that pure friendship between two beings with whom God always makes a third.

Louise had first to pass through a period of uncertainties, of groping, retracing of steps, the nursing and healing of those old wounds of her spirit which had re-opened. First of all material questions had to be settled. The long illness and the unsatisfactory stewardship of her husband had almost ruined the family. Monsieur Gachier owed her a substantial sum: but she could not obtain payment. She was in fact once again almost reduced to living on her two pensions, which were small enough. She therefore gave up living at the Hôtel du Marais, which she decided to make over to her son, and retired to a modest apartment in the Saint-Victor district, which brought her very close to the Collège des Bons Enfants, where Monsieur Vincent had just started the 'Mission', and also to that great group of Parisian seventeenth-century schools and colleges, where her son, still backward and difficult, would be able to make his studies.

We can form some impression of what we may call her years of widowhood (1625-1629) from the few letters out of her correspondence with Monsieur Vincent which have been preserved. Of these the greater part, but not all, have now been published.

She manifests great impatience and would like to undertake work of some kind, but does not know what the work should be. Her director restrains her, moderating and calming her impulsiveness. This was always his way, to transpose to the supernatural plane the maxim, 'Wait and see'. Let her first work upon herself and put a brake upon her eagerness; let her take account of her errors when she has detected them, and remove their cause; let her live her life of widowhood to the full—for she had renewed, immediately after the death of her husband, her vow of widowhood.

Here then she lived in her apartment, attended by a single servant girl, whom she desired to be pious and silent. She had wanted to live alone, yet she always felt the oppression of solitude, and the sense of obscurity which goes with it and holds so many dangers. She found a refuge in her director and attached herself to him as to a saviour. She was able to see him frequently, since he lived close at hand. But he was fully occupied with his country mission in the environs of Paris. He was often away evangelising some country district belonging to the Gondi family, and his absences were long. Louise was desperate, driven to distraction. To Camus, bishop of Belley, who continued to be a friend and close confidant, though at a distance, she made known the troubles of her mind, only to receive from him a somewhat sharp reprimand.

'Pardon me, my very dear sister, if I tell you that you are inclined to attach yourself a little too much to those who direct you and you lean on them a little too heavily. Behold, Monsieur Vincent is now eclipsed, and Mlle Le

Gras is out of humour, she has lost her bearings and is bewildered. It is very necessary to see God in our guides and directors and to look at them as they are in God; but sometimes it is necessary to look at God only, for he can cure our paralysis and other disorders without the help of man and without any new immersion. As to your retreat, take advice about it from some good spiritual father such as Père Menard of the Oratory, or of Reverend Mother Magdalen, or else of Mother Superior of the Visitation, and then go to your retreat with confidence. It is not, dear soul, that it is burdensome to me to guide and counsel you: alas! no. On the contrary, I hope that by doing as I say you will raise me up to heaven, where your example stimulates me more than my advice can help you to find the way there. But it is in this spirit that my dear Mlle Le Gras, whom I esteem so highly and who seems to me to be so enlightened and so strong, should abide. I do not care to see in her these little weaknesses, nor these little clouds upon her spirit.

26th July.

Camus is ready to set her an example in detachment and is prepared to send her back if necessary to Monsieur Vincent himself:

My daughter, it is not for love of you that I go tomorrow to Montmartre, nor for Mlle Chaundlin's good girl, whom I chose yesterday, but only to have the pleasure of waiting upon Monsieur Vincent in his own house; and if I believed it possible that he would not be there or that you should not wish to let us return, just our two selves, on foot as far as Saint-Lazare, I would not wish to go. Let me know, Mademoiselle, your resolve; it will be the stronger when I am with you, that resolve of yours.

With her new director Louise was more reserved, but she complained of being neglected and miserable.

5th June, 1627.

Monsieur,

I hope that you will pardon the liberty that I take in communicating to you the impatience of my mind, as much for the long interval that has passed as for apprehension about the future, and not to know to what place you are going when you leave the place where you are. It is true, Father, that the thought of the matter which is taking you away does a little to sweeten my sadness, but that does not prevent the days from sometimes seeming like months to me in my present idle condition. However, I desire to await in peace the hour of God and I recognise that it is only my unworthiness which postpones it. . . .

Monsieur Vincent did not want to be harsh with her or push her along too fast. He apologised for having gone away without telling her, to save her grief at seeing him go so suddenly. But it is evident that his strategy was deliberate, to make her get used to the guidance of her own life, and to putting herself completely in the hands of Providence.

The time had come when, if she were to be fit to undertake in the future tasks which might be tough and heavy, she must form in herself a robust and virile spirit free from womanly softness. He rebuked her constant agitation about her son. 'If you are a woman of spirit, you will rid yourself of your little diversions and motherly sensitivities. I have never seen a mother who was more a mother than you. In no other respect are you so much a woman as in this.' The word *amusements*, which Monsieur Vincent here uses, is a little hard, but he was to soften its force in later years by the solicitude he himself displayed for the apathetic and unstable Michel.

Her daily occupations were those of a lady of rank who was escaping from the world to train herself for Heaven. She attended to her household duties, received and paid a few infrequent visits, prayed and meditated, and 'amused' herself according to her tastes and aptitudes. She painted water-colour studies of sacred subjects and, now that she had the leisure, took up painting in oil. It is probably to this period that we may attribute her large oil paintings, of which the best known and best authenticated is the *Seigneur de la Charité*. She painted it at this time, between 1625 and 1628. It represents Christ, the Lord of Charity, who loves mankind and commands men to love one another and to relieve the wretched. The workmanship is robust, if a little immature, and the expression of the features of an imperious sweetness. One detail in this picture has given rise to a controversy which has not yet been satisfactorily settled: in place of the heart of flesh, the heart is in some way luminous, a kind of stain of fire beneath the linen robe. This feature has led some to believe that Louise had some conception of the devotion to the Sacred Heart, as did St Jean Eudes, before the revelation to St Margaret Mary. This is not very likely. Neither in her recorded words nor in her writings do we find any trace of this particular devotion. But it is certainly noteworthy that, by a pious intuition, she should have had the idea of representing Christ's love for men by the luminous transparency of his heart.

She did some sewing and knitting for the poor, and Monsieur Vincent levied from her a contribution, just as he did from Mlle Du Fay: send three shirts to Mlle De Lamoignon; five or six shirts for Palaiseau. . . . She worked at religious ornaments, made vestments for the chapel at St Lazare. Monsieur Vincent sent her his thanks—perhaps he realised how much she had once needed tenderness—in exquisite words which must have touched her to the heart.

The grace of our Lord be with you for ever.

This note has three purposes: to greet you, to thank you for this very beautiful and comfortable frontal which your charity has sent to us. Yesterday it overwhelmed my heart with joy to see your heart therein, as I entered the chapel, all of a sudden, not knowing that the frontal was

there; my joy lasted all yesterday and I feel it still with an
inexplicable tenderness which arouses in me several
ideas; if God sees fit, I shall be able to tell you what these
ideas are, being content meanwhile to tell you that I beg
of God to adorn your soul with his perfect and holy love,
since you thus adorn his house with so many beautiful
vestments. . . .

This is not his usual tone. Monsieur Vincent was affectionate, but reserved and serious even in his smiles. One of the
erasures in a letter written by him shows us both the sensitivity of his heart and the resourcefulness of his pedagogy.
What he had written was: 'I am, with all the tenderness of
my affection, in the love of our Lord, your . . .'; he has
scratched out 'with all the tenderness of my affection', it
remains legible, but is compensated for by the erasure which
re-establishes the spiritual tone.

In this sort of life, spiritual work becomes a necessity.
Always impatient, her mind still full of complications, Louise
shut herself up in a rule of life and a multitude of pious
practices with not the slightest place for personal liberty or
for that spiritual imagination which is so refreshing to the
human spirit. Her rule is a model of mechanical living, carefully contrived. From five in the morning—soon she was to
make it from four in the morning—until eight in the evening,
every hour, every quarter hour, became a pigeon-hole into
which was inserted a prayer, a meditation, some pious
practice, activities which varied according to the day of the
week. Into this framework—and with how many difficulties
—are inserted the religious exercises proper to the nine or ten
confraternities to which she has given her name, and acts of
piety for the satisfaction of her personal devotion, such as the
thirty-three acts of piety which she had devised in honour
of the thirty-three years of the life of our Lord. The object
of a rule of life is to sustain and strengthen the will, not to
confine it in an iron collar; but this woman, without the
protection of the enclosure of a convent, without the aid of

conventual discipline, is always the victim of scruples, which add their weight to that of the law. Other biographers of Louise de Marillac have admired this heroism; I cannot do so, since it does not lead her to the joy that should be found in love.

Monsieur Vincent did not launch a frontal attack, but rallied her gently about her over-eager disposition, begging her not to load herself with rules and practices and not to scruple to omit some of those which she had laid down for herself. He was also at pains to moderate her austerities, her disciplinary practices, and her fasting, which would only have ended by ruining a health already delicate. He begged her to take care of herself so that she could be of service later. 'Go patiently, go prudently, be as happy as you can.'

This was what she lacked most. She knew nothing of joy. Since infancy nothing had caused her spirit to expand— neither marriage nor motherhood had brought her true happiness, and her religion was no better than the rest. She was sad and depressed; she lived by rigid discipline to an heroic degree, yet she was sad: a subtle form of neurasthenia had imprisoned her in its grip.

She was very anxious to escape from this frustrated state and do something. But what could she do? Enter a convent? Monsieur Vincent did not push her in that direction. He was waiting for circumstances which could be taken as signs of the will of God. These signs soon came. Louise had noted the direction taken by Monsieur Vincent's Mission, which tended always to the relief of the sufferings of the poor through local Charities. It was to this way of serving the poor that she came to devote her life. Her decision was taken and she told him of it. Here at last was the sign which they had both sought for so long. Monsieur Vincent was overjoyed:

1628(?)

Yes, at last, my dear Demoiselle, I sincerely desire it; why not? Since our Lord has given you this holy desire.

Will you therefore communicate tomorrow, and prepare yourself for the salutary self-examination which you suggest, and after that you will commence the holy exercises which you have drawn up for yourself. I cannot express to you how ardently my heart desires to see you and to know how this thing has come to pass in your heart, but I wish to mortify this desire in myself for the love of God, with which love I also desire that your heart should be wholly occupied. Now, I can imagine that the words of the Gospel for today must have touched you very much. In this way they are always present to the loving heart which loves to perfection. Oh, what a beautiful tree must you appear today to be, in the eyes of God, since you have produced such fruit! May you for ever more be a tree of beauty, a tree of life, producing the fruits of love, and may I be so too, in this same love.

V.D.

JOURNEYINGS FOR CHARITY

HER new life began with a retreat; its framework and the subjects for prayer were set down by her director. Louise had only to follow the lines laid down by him and to give him an account of her progress everyday. He was anxious to know whether it was indeed God who had spoken and he wanted her to be quite sure of herself. As with every other retreat prepared by Monsieur Vincent, these conferences recalled the retreatant to the fundamentals of Christianity: imitation of the life of Christ, submission to the will of God, an active struggle with self-love; with the most concise of resolutions, kept well within what was possible. The retreatant faithfully wrote down the course of her meditations and the 'light' that she received in making them. She had done this throughout her life on her two retreats each year, at Advent and Pentecost. The Daughters of Charity have preserved these intimate records. Unfortunately, few of the notes bear any indication of the date; others are dated only approximately. But they form a treasury of spiritual writing to which I shall return in a later chapter, since they should not be regarded as applicable only to the year 1625 or 1629. The effusion of grace was not limited to one outpouring: it had been sufficient to the occasion, so that the retreatant felt herself well armed for her new way of life. Louise was about to emerge from her solitude. She was to engage in personal activity, to assume responsibilities; and she would find in them what she had sought: the healing of that malady which had afflicted her from birth. She was at last on the point of attaining self-realisation and expansion of mind and spirit.

Monsieur Vincent had wound up all his country missions in order to concentrate upon establishing 'the Charity' in Paris. Before, he had preached the Gospel; now he set about practising it. He sent out a summons to the ladies of the aristocracy living in the parish, to women of the middle class and to any working-class wives and girls who were better off than their neighbours. He invited them to form an association for the regular care of the sick and assistance of the poor. Every form of misery was to be solaced on the spot by this union of all social classes in one Christian community.

Years before, in 1617, while working at Châtillon-les-Dombes, Monsieur Vincent had drawn up the Rule for the first of his Charities. It is a monument of tenderness and good sense, in which everything is foreseen, yet which leaves the way open for future development and adaptation. The highly technical details keep a manner and tone which are maternal:

> 'She who is on duty for the day', says the Rule, 'will bring in the dinner and carry it to the sick; as she enters, she will greet the patient cheerfully and charitably. She will set the bed-table over the bed, and put a cloth on the table, with a platter, a spoon and bread; she will wash the hands of the patient, and say grace; she will pour soup into a bowl and put meat on a plate, arranging everything on the said bed-table. She will then charitably invite the patient to eat, for the love of Jesus and his holy Mother; and she will do all things lovingly, as though for her own son, or rather for God, who will accept as done to himself the good she does to the poor. She will address to him in this sense some few words concerning our Lord, seeking to cheer him, if he be very depressed; she will sometimes cut up his meat for him, and pour out his drink; and having settled him down to his meal, if he have someone else at hand, she will leave this patient, and go on her way, to find another to be likewise treated; remembering always to begin with those that are attended and to end with those who are alone, so that she may remain with these for a longer time.'

The Charities had multiplied under his hands in the

country districts round about Paris. In the early stages development had been rapid, but now there was falling away here and there. Each Charity was introducing methods of its own and too much diversity was ruining the very spirit of the foundation. It had become necessary to visit the Charities, to institute a strict enquiry, to reform and to correct. The Charities had come into being: and now it was Charity that had to be defended.

'Go then, as from God', was the mandate given to Louise de Marillac. She left Paris in May 1629.

It was a strange undertaking for a woman of society. Accompanied by one of her friends or by a servant girl, she went at her own expense, by the public coach, facing all the uncertainties and hazards of the road, getting down at the roadside inns like any other traveller. But Louise went farther afield than other travellers—into the hamlets and hovels away from the main roads. When, because of the poor roads, she could no longer go by coach she would take to horseback and go on. Her personal luggage was of the lightest, but her large wicker basket was stuffed with linen, clothing, medicines, sedatives and comforts. It was her happiness to be able to 'refresh', with a clean shirt, some badly neglected invalid and give him a little of the joy which is felt by the disinherited when they receive something 'extra' and unexpected.

Upon arrival in the villages she would put up at the hostelry, seek out the members of the Charity, call a meeting in one of their houses, and see how things were with them. Here her natural aptitudes, developed by her years with 'the poor Demoiselle' and by her responsibilities in her husband's home, at last found their outlet. The records taken during these visits have been preserved. They are objective and precise. This particular Charity has a 'reserve capital' of no more than three *écus*; that one has incurred debts; here, there are six sheep and eight lambs; elsewhere, there is no regular

visiting of the sick; in another place, the Daughters themselves
are becoming lax about their spiritual duties; here and there,
rivalries and jealousies among the Daughters are spoiling
everything.

The enquiry completed, Louise issued directives. Then, if
possible, she gathered the women and girls together again, for
an exhortation to piety and mutual love. One of her greatest
concerns was to know whether there was any woman in the
village who could teach children to read; if there was
nobody who could undertake it, Louise would take steps to
provide someone. In her eyes this elementary education was
part of the duty of charity. Within four years, Louise visited
in this way all the Charities in the environs of Paris, travelling during the winter months as well as in the dry season.
Montmirail, Asnières, St Cloud, Villepreux, St-Germain,
Verneuil were all inspected and invigorated. Then she went
further afield to Beauvais, to the villages of Champagne and
into Burgundy. She arranged and rearranged, she soothed,
she imparted a new zeal. The information she brought to
Monsieur Vincent was of inestimable value to him, for he
was often ignorant of how things had gone since his departure;
and of course all this was of the greatest practical use to
Louise herself as her work took shape. She was touching the
depths of human wretchedness and of the resources of
charity, the two things most essential to all active love, all
fruitful work for mankind.

In the acquisition of this knowledge Louise had to walk
upon thorns. She was not long in meeting those who turned a
jaundiced eye upon good works. In one place some public
official—the village constable, as he might be today—
denounced her to the authorities as 'engaging in subversive
activities'; in more than one parish the curate complained
that this woman, who went about catechising the girls, was
usurping his own functions! At Châlons the Bishop himself
was inclined to be hostile to this woman, who had descended
upon his diocese like a delegate whose mandate, at any rate

in matters spiritual, he was resolved not to recognise. Monsieur Vincent advised Mlle de Marillac always to give a frank account of herself and her mission and if her explanation was not accepted, to withdraw with good grace and go back home. For the rest, none of her travelling experience was wasted and after the adventure with the Bishop of Châlons, preliminary negotiations were regularly opened with the commissaries, bishops and parish clergy before the launching of any new mission.

Trials of this kind were scarcely to be avoided: any missionary with a novel appeal will meet both with defiance and with enthusiasm. It sometimes happened that when Louise de Marillac ended a mission she would be led out of the place in procession and acclaimed as a benefactress sent by God. We may well believe that her spirit, as yet lacking in this kind of experience, was highly sensitive to these variations in public opinion, just as her poor constitution was ill-adapted to the sudden changes of temperature so characteristic of the Ile de France. The lash of icy winds reduced her face to plainness, and she had to make up her mind to wear a mask for the protection of her skin, such as the great ladies of the day wore to make themselves attractive. This mask or veil was indispensable to her on her journeys, and it inspired the distinctive feature of the habit of the Daughters of Charity, the stiff linen hood which was later substituted for the original peasant-girl *coiffe*.

Absorbed though she was in this new activity of travelling, yet she could not all at once detach herself from that other world in which the family of de Marillac was carving itself a flourishing career.

In 1626 Michel de Marillac became Keeper of the Seals, then Chancellor of France, to embark shortly afterwards upon reform of French law. Louis de Marillac received a marshal's *baton* and the command of the armies which were about to cross the Alps and march into Italy. There was even a day when a Marillac overthrew the mighty Richelieu and occupied his place in the King's council. But within twenty-four hours Richelieu was again in power, and on November 16th, 1630, he ordered the arrest of Michel, who had been minister of state for one short day, and had him put in prison. The Marshal Louis he had arrested at the head of his troops, and a special court set up to conduct his trial. From this day forth Louise lived through the tragedy with his wife, who in the end died of despair. The Marshal was eventually beheaded on May 10th, 1632. The fall of that illustrious head made a great noise in Europe, and struck with a dull weight upon the heart of Louise.

It is from Vincent de Paul's letters that we learn of her emotions at this time. Her letters to him are now lost, but we may well suppose that her feelings would bring her back with a submissive heart to the will of God.

'The news you have sent me concerning the Maréchal de Marillac seems to me deserving of very great compassion. Let us adore in this event the good pleasure of God, and the happy state of those who by patience in their own sorrows venerate the sufferings of the Son of God. It matters not to us how our relatives go to God, provided they go to him indeed. Now, the customary observances of this manner of death give the best warrant of eternal life. Let us not therefore complain, but let us accept the adorable will of God.'

These tragic events did not distract her from her work: visiting and organising the Charities in summer, and during the winter months establishing the Charities in the parishes of Paris. Before long there was one in every parish of Paris.

During these four years of activity, a great change took place in her. She had at last broken the fetters of her debility. Much of her time was now spent in the open air. Sometimes fatigue broke down her strength. But she had learnt what she could prudently undertake and how far she could exert herself with her frail health. Her mind had cleared and had learnt simplicity. She saw life as it was and not in the distorting mirror of her imagination. She had always been very dependent upon her director, but now that she had often to be away from him, and alone, she was learning to make her own decisions. She had learnt the power of the spoken word. The women of the Charities loved to listen to Louise, and the men concealed themselves about the place so that they too might have the pleasure of hearing her discourses. She had discovered that responsive moment when religion can be introduced to the uncouth minds of the country people and appeal to the needs, if not to the longings, of their hearts. Her relations with God were no longer impeded by scruples or by fear. Of necessity and with joy she was founding her devotion upon that liberty which is love.

In short, those four years of activity worked a cure in her. True, she had still to reckon with an occasional attack of the old neurosis, but the malady had yielded to the treatment. This was a grace from God. Humanly speaking it was the work of Monsieur Vincent, not in the sense that he had formed in her a new character, but in the sense that it was he who helped her to find herself. What he brought her was not so much a doctrine as a method. She was now relieved of the heavy anxieties of her childhood and youth. She had exorcised the curse laid upon her, as once she had believed, in her cradle. She resumed now, in the light of a new day, in the light of a liberated love of God, all the rights which were hers as a member of society. She was a Marillac, of that race which had always stood level with glory, defeat and death. Whether with deliberate intent, or by instinct, she began to use again the proud name of Marillac, dropping once for all her husband's family name. All her letters henceforward are signed 'Louise de Marillac', and it is noteworthy that the Church canonised her, not by the name which was hers by marriage, but by the name which had been given her by her father.

She had now reached the age of forty and had emerged from a long nightmare. Her personality was completely her own. Let us see what she did with it.

PART II

THE GREAT ACCOMPLISHMENT

HOW THE WORK BEGAN

IN THE course of her long journeys through the countryside, by coach, horseback or foot, and in the streets of the towns, Louise de Marillac had thrown off her past and had begun to make a study of the present. For her, 'the present' meant the work of the Charities, and she had arrived at the conviction that these could only survive if they were served by women attached to them permanently and by vocation.

Well-intentioned women tired of the work; married women were pre-occupied with their families and their housekeeping; fashionable ladies could not bring themselves to 'carry the soup through the streets to the houses of the poor'; they began to depute that duty to their servants; visits to the sick began to be less regular: the ladies slipped into an easy substitute for sick-visiting, and gave alms instead of giving themselves. The real need was for servants who would give themselves.

Whether it was Louise or Monsieur Vincent who came to the idea first is of little consequence. It was a thought from the mind of God—and before long, servants were offering themselves. Wherever Louise found a good girl who was ready to devote herself to the sick and the poor, she would set her to work, observing and guiding her from a distance. This was how she discovered that inspiring personality, Marguerite Nasau, a cow-girl from a remote village and a true daughter of charity before the Daughters of Charity came into existence. She gave herself to charity; taught herself to read, getting help with her alphabet from passers-by, that she might perform the same charity for other children. She devoted herself to the most thankless tasks among the afflicted and died of the plague, contracted while nursing poor victims of the scourge in Marseilles.

There is a logic of dedication. The Charity had need of devoted servants, but no servant could be useful without some training for her duties; the girls must have technical, moral and spiritual preparation; they must be directed; they must have something to eat, somewhere to live.

Therefore, a Congregation must be founded. The word had an awe-inspiring sound and the matter was certainly a weighty one. Louise was a woman in a hurry, eager to move the work forward, but Vincent held her back. Most certainly he would have agreed with the opinion expressed by Michel de Marillac—how many years before?—that we should never seek to constrain God to grant us more graces than he wishes us to have. But at length Monsieur Vincent sanctioned an attempt.

The four or five volunteers who had offered themselves were brought together and Louise established them in her own rooms. It was November 20th, 1633. By March 25th, 1634, the infant community had acquired such stability that the foundress, who was by this time in a very great hurry, bound herself by vow to consecrate herself entirely and without reserve to this work.

About the beginning of all great works undertaken in complete simplicity for the will of God there is a freshness, the freshness of childhood. Monsieur Vincent lived very near; he came often and in grave and familiar words talked to the peasant girls as though they were duchesses. Louise poured out upon them the accumulated treasure of her heart.

This does not mean that life went by with perfect smoothness in those cramped quarters. These country maidens were without education even of the most elementary kind. Most of them could not even read. Difficulties were encountered: mutual love and encouragement, the politenesses of charity, the life of prayer, mortification, had to be learnt until they became habitual. One or two of the volunteers rebelled and went back home, but others came in their stead. There were scenes, storms of complaint, scolding and tears and bursts of laughter. Yet gradually order and serenity were established. There could be no question of giving these girls a rule of the kind suited to nuns; they would make do with statutes as substitute for a rule. Louise drew up the statutes and Monsieur Vincent thought them excellent. In July, 1634, he came to read them to the 'Sisters', now twelve in number. His commentary upon the statutes was greatly moving. Every one of the girls accepted them with complete faith. All fell upon their knees and promised to keep the laws of the community. The Holy Spirit had descended and Vincent and Louise knelt and gave thanks. We may look back to that day as the foundation-day of the community of the Daughters of Charity.

The house in the rue St Victor had to be enlarged to receive all the postulants who began to come in from the villages. The Foundress and her director did not attempt to recruit from any urban or middle-class area: it is difficult for these classes to stoop to the lowly services which some kinds of sickness demand. But Monsieur Vincent and Louise could rightly value the stalwart spirit of the village girls. He describes them with pride and we catch from his words a certain perfume, as of the memories of his own boyhood.

True country girls are extremely simple. They do not make use of subtleties of speech, nor words with a double meaning. They are not obstinately attached to their own opinions, nor to getting their own way, and they believe with great simplicity whatever people tell them. These are the points in which you must imitate them: for you will truly be Daughters of Charity if you are entirely simple and are not obstinate as to your own opinions; if you willingly give way to the wishes of other people; if you are candid in your speech, not saying one thing and thinking something different. I would like to believe that all this applies to you. God be praised, my daughters!

We may observe in true country girls a great degree of

humility. They never glory in their possessions; they do not talk about how well connected they are; they do not regard themselves as having cultivated minds, they walk about modestly; and although some may be better off than other girls, they do not therefore live better than the rest, but they all live on equal terms together. Generally speaking, this is not the case with the girls of the towns, who are always talking about their houses, their relations, the things they possess: and very often they will boast of having things which in point of fact they have not. The Daughters of Charity should be very far removed from the spirit of town girls; and it does seem to me that, by the grace of God, they are indeed very far removed from it.

These country girls had to be formed by him. Most of them learned to read, so that they would be able to teach children to read; and to write, so that they would be able to send in written reports of their doings to Mademoiselle. The older girls were taught how to bleed a patient and when proficient they were entrusted with lancets. All had to know the everyday remedies and the ordinary ways of using them. The rough-and-ready nature of this training makes the modern reader smile; but it was a great advance on the methods used by the voluntary nurses of the time, who adhered firmly to traditional remedies which were of doubtful value.

Their training in religion was more thorough. Louise made it her first care to instruct them carefully, to send them out as good Christians. They had to know their catechism and put it into practice. Then through meditation they were led to a fuller spiritual life. The virtues, and particularly those essential to the vocation of Charity, were grafted on to faith and the love of God. They were taught the habit of mutual support and help which is indispensable to the stability of a community, and acquired a sympathetic understanding of the conditions of life of the sick and the poor, to whose service they were called. They were taught that the poor man comes

first in the Church: he is prince and master there, for he is a
sort of incarnation of Christ. He must therefore be ministered
to with respect, whatever his character and his faults; and
he must be loved. The sick man is a suffering member of the
Body of Christ and he is therefore to be touched only with
reverence. As to the care of his body, he is often, alas! no
more capable of looking after himself than a child—and
always the sick man is like a child in mind: illness makes him
feeble and irritable, the slightest clumsiness offends him and
the most fleeting of smiles will fill his heart with joy.

Thus equipped, and clad in a new dress of grey serge—
they came to be called 'the grey sisters'—and hooded in the
white toque of the country districts, their feet firmly settled
in stout clogs, the Daughters of Charity went wherever they
were wanted—and they were very much in demand—and
wherever they were sent.

Their duties were very precisely laid down for them. They
were servants. They began as servants to the high-born ladies
who ministered to the poor and through them, by virtue of
their duty of obedience, they were themselves servants of the
poor. This was the guiding principle. A guiding principle it
has always remained, although the turn of events very soon
put upon it new interpretations. The Ladies of Charity,
especially in the towns, found it natural to delegate to the
Daughters most of the active work of the Charity, of which
they themselves retained the control and the credit—and
also, we are bound to say, the financial burden. With the
passage of time the control exercised by the Ladies became
nominal: they supplied the funds and presided at the
meetings; and thus the Daughters, who began as 'servants'
of the Charities, became in fact servants of the poor. Between
the Ladies and the Daughters there was occasional friction
and conflict. This was to be expected. But such petty things
do not make the true stuff of life, and in truth the Ladies
by their persevering generosity and the Daughters by their
heroic devotion wrote the history of that age, to such good

purpose that we may well ask whether without them France
could have borne its sorrows.

The Charities established in the parishes of Paris asked the
help of the Daughters so that they could continue to function.
'You are in demand everywhere! Just imagine!' Monsieur
Vincent said, not without a touch of affectionate irony
'Good-natured servants content with little in the way of
board and lodging—the whole world is looking for them!'
They were also in demand at the Hôtel-Dieu.

In this vast hospital, the oldest and largest in Paris, had
been established another charity of a very different kind. It
was administered by the Canons of Notre-Dame, and no
stones need be thrown at them, nor at the nursing staff, who
were Augustinian nuns. Yet it has to be admitted that neither
the nuns nor the Canons allowed themselves to be overwhelmed by the ever-increasing multitude of patients
crowding into the inadequate premises, overtaxing the
antiquated hospital equipment. Reduced to bare necessities,
the patients lacked almost everything and grumbled constantly. Certain ladies of rank, touched with pity for their
condition, expressed a desire to cheer the patients by regular
visits, enlivening conversation and little gifts of extra food
and comforts. Among these were Madame la Présidente
Goussault, Madame la Présidente de Herse, Mme Fouquet,
Mme de Traversay, Charlotte de Montmorency, la duchesse
d'Aiguillon, Marie de Gonzague, la duchesse de Ventadour
and . . . Mlle Le Gras.

Monsieur Vincent was consulted. At first he hesitated,
reluctant to risk offending the Augustinian nuns and the
Canons of Notre-Dame. But in the end, when every anxiety
had been soothed, he gave way, called the noble ladies
together, set up a new confraternity and drew up a Rule.
There was much enthusiasm. All the great ladies of the
capital wanted to enrol and it was wonderful to see them,
each on her appointed day, put on the white blouse and make
the round of the wards, followed by the Daughters of Mlle

Le Gras. The girls carried large baskets from which they distributed cakes and jellies to the sick, exhorting them to make good confessions and get up as soon as possible.

This book is not a history of the Ladies of Charity, an organisation which appears and re-appears in the history of the Daughters. But it deserves to be put on record that their sick-visiting at the Hôtel-Dieu, though it began as a fashionable recreation, was the source of great things. The ladies of the French aristocracy came into direct contact with human misery and accustomed themselves to solace the wretched. This education in social services stood them in good stead in future years, when they formed that great host of charitable workers mobilised by Monsieur Vincent and Louise de Marillac to save France from famine during the tragedy of the Thirty Years' War. Perhaps never before in the history of France had there been such vast depths of human suffering and never had charity achieved so much. If misery did not at this time find an outlet in revolution, it was only because at the moment the dykes were ready to burst they were reinforced by that very goodness which wretchedness had called into activity.

But I am anticipating. In the rue St Victor the original premises could no longer hold all the daughters. They would have to move. Moreover, Monsieur Vincent had left the Collège de Bons Enfants and now lived in the priory of St Lazare, at the other end of Paris. Both the young community and the Foundress had need of him and they would have to move if they were to be near him: not too near, perhaps—it was his own advice—but within reach. Finding an empty house not far from St Lazare in the village of La Chapelle, on the way to St Denis, Mademoiselle and her fifteen Daughters moved into it in May, 1636.

The youthful anxieties of the community was now at an end. Its adult life had begun.

EXPANSION

THE HOUSE at La Chapelle was in the open country, but cramped and inconvenient and too far from the centre of Paris. The community stayed less than three years. In 1641 the Daughters established themselves with more elbow-room in the St Laurent district, opposite the priory of St Lazare. The house was first bought by the Mission and then resold to the Daughters of Charity, when they had acquired legal status. At last arrangements could be made for the long-term organisation of all their many activities. They could plan for the future with confidence, as can a man who is at last conscious of dwelling in a home of his own.

The Congregation developed with a controlled rapidity, prudently kept in hand by the foundress. Calls for help were answered only within the limits which the rate of recruitment made advisable. In many districts the Ladies of Charity were themselves the principal 'recruiting sergeants'; since they were working for their own Charities they searched zealously for vocations. Mademoiselle stood in no need of Monsieur Vincent's cautious warnings when it came to sorting out the postulants: by temperament and experience she was a prudent woman. In the first place, she rejected all melancholy applicants out of hand and on principle: a girl had to have a robust and cheerful mind if she were not to succumb to the sadness which lay like a marsh vapour over the misery of the poor and sick. Louise was also on her guard against those discontented country girls whose only vocation was a desire for change. And she distrusted those flighty maidens who were ready to answer a call if it gave them an opportunity to travel and, above all, to see Paris. She demanded a firmly-grounded vocation, a desire to serve God, the sick and the poor. Candidates were only to leave their homes for Paris with the consent of their parents and furnished with a recommendation from their parish priest. They must come with a new outfit of clothes and with a sum of money sufficient to pay for the journey to Paris and home again—for some after trying the life might not want to stay, and others might be asked to depart. It was simply commonsense to come provided.

Once the postulant was accepted she entered the novitiate. The rules which governed this period were not formulated all at once. To bring into harmony the religious life of perfection and the life of a nurse dependent at every moment on the claims of others was no easy matter. A balance was eventually found, as we shall see, but for the moment the focus was on essentials.

Scarcely were the first girls trained when a period of rapid expansion began.

Louise de Marillac's vision had been clear. The Charities needed women devoted to the cause, who would have no purpose in life but to dedicate themselves and bring about the dedication of others. For their work to have lasting effect they must be firmly established; they must be established in community, because it is not humanly possible to live the life of a servant in isolation. So at first it was a matter of laying true foundations.

This was easy in the parishes of Paris, where the organisation was at first a sort of compromise between the older type of charitable confraternity and the new developments. Then centres were formed in the suburbs on the same model, but these soon found it better to set themselves up as proper foundations. The first suburban foundation was at St Germain-en-Laye which began modestly as auxiliary work to the hospital in 1638. The second foundation was at Richelieu, in 1639. Richelieu was only a small town, but it belonged to Mlle de Combalet, niece of the Cardinal, later duchesse d'Aiguillon, a lady of high rank who was very zealous for the Mission and for all the good works of Vincent

de Paul. We could almost say that the foundation at Richelieu
got special attention and the most capable of the girls were
sent there to please so eminent a patroness.

Le Mans, where priests of the Mission had been working
for some years, requested the help of Louise de Marillac's
Daughters. Right from the start, Louise and Monsieur
Vincent had decided certain basic conditions for any new
foundation, their object being to protect the spiritual
autonomy and smooth working of all their houses. When it
proved impossible to reach a working compromise with the
'Fathers of the Poor' in Le Mans, the Daughters, who had
arrived and were about to begin work, packed their bags
and returned to Paris.

It was less difficult for the community to find work in
Angers. This foundation was due to the zeal of Madame la
présidente Goussault. Here the Daughters embarked upon a
new form of active work which was no longer a simple labour
of charity. The magistrates and 'The Fathers of the Poor'
requested the Daughters to take over the hospital and run it
on their own; it was a large hospital with two hundred beds
in regular use, so we are told. To decide a matter of this
magnitude, Louise set out from Paris with her group of girls.
She reached Angers after a journey of fourteen days by coach
and by barge, and drew up a contract with the magistrates
which bears all the marks of her organising ability and that
gift of foresight which could insert into regulations all sorts
of provisions for the settlement of future difficulties. She found
providential help on the spot in the person of the Vicar
General of Angers, the Abbé de Vaux, who became the firm
friend of the community, its protector and affectionate guide.
He was a man of warm heart and enlightened intelligence,
self-effacing in the careless style of the aristocrat. He understood Louise and felt that he was understood by her, and
this complete and tacit mutual sympathy enhanced the
efficacy of all that he did to promote the welfare and sustain
the fervour of the Charity in Angers. In this city there were

never any 'incidents' in the Charity, and it set a noble
example to the Charities elsewhere.

In the midst of all the fatigues and celebration incidental
to launching the Daughters in Angers, Mademoiselle was
suddenly stricken with illness. The news reached Paris,
growing more exaggerated on the journey. There was great
alarm. Monsieur Vincent, ordinarily the calmest of men,
wrote letter upon letter. He urged Louise to return to Paris
by coach or by litter and to take all possible care of a health
so necessary to the service of God.

From 1641 to 1660, Louise wrote almost every week to her
Daughters at Angers. When she read their letters to her, she
could live with them the events they described; when she
wrote to them, she could share with them the daily life of the
mother-house, and in a way her own personal life too, so
great and so contagious was the spontaneous warmth of her
heart. Let us listen for a moment to that voice, at once so
firm and so tender, so scolding and yet so sweet, which could
make her presence felt over any distance. She is writing in
1643 to the sisters at Angers. Even in a community so fervent
as this, discord and even coquetry could work mischief.
Louise hears something of the kind and writes forcefully:

'Can it be possible that any attachment to creatures
should put us in peril of losing the great treasure of our
vocation? Take good care, my dear sisters, for the danger
is noxious, because people do not suspect that vanity may
lurk beneath our poor habits and ugly hoods. Unless we
are careful, there will be, beneath an appearance of
breeding and propriety, grave faults in this matter. I do
not wish to believe that any of you, my very dear sisters,
should give place to a single thought which is contrary
to your holy vocation, nor that you should dare to take
pleasure in speaking to anyone who could do any damage
to the purity of the love you should have for God. For
God is jealous for the souls which he calls into his holy

service. If some of you have had some little touches of this passion, O my very dear sisters, do not let the viper lodge in your bosom. Disclose the thoughts of your heart to him whom God has given you as a director, who is the person that M. l'Abbé de Vaux has appointed to hear you. God will not fail to comfort and assist you in the matter. . . .'

The renown of the hospital at Angers aroused the interest of the 'Fathers of the Poor' in Nantes. Their enormous hospital, full of intricate corridors and staircases, old, ill-fitted and ill-kept, was a great anxiety to them. The 'Fathers' paid a visit of inspection to Angers, they asked questions and looked into things carefully. Then they declared that they, too, would like to have the Daughters of Charity. Before giving them an answer, Mademoiselle concentrated her attention upon the hospital at St Denis, which her dear friends Mlle de Lamoignon and Mme de Nesmond had desired. When the project at Nantes began to take shape, she decided that she would go herself and inaugurate the new foundation. This was quite an expedition and it was organised to the last degree. The duties of the mother-house were distributed for her period of absence with a wealth of proviso and delegated powers such as the Sisters of today recall with a certain amusement, as they set out for the Far East and the New World.

Louise has herself left us a description of this journey. It was hard and wearisome, yet picturesque, and in some of its details not unlike a holiday tour. We gather from her words that it was made with much eagerness and devotion and with the courage and confidence of a young girl. Trials there would be in plenty, but the venture began with anticipations of triumph. It will be of interest to produce this record in full. Students of our past will discover from it what it was like to travel, in the year 1646, from Paris to Orleans, and then from Orleans to Nantes by way of the river Loire. It is written joyously, in clear straightforward language. Students of psychology will examine the account for evidence concerning the effects of travelling upon morale. For many years of her life, Louise de Marillac had been of a melancholy turn; indeed, I have in an earlier chapter described her condition as neurasthenia. Her cure was still of recent date, and she still occasionally suffered attacks of sadness and anxiety. Yet now, from the moment of leaving for Nantes, she tells us that she was very cheerful and that she was able to bear with good humour the incidents of the road:

'On Thursday, the 26th day of July, by the grace of God we left Paris in the company of our dear sisters Elisabeth, Claude, Marguerite Noret, Catherine Bagard, Perrette of Sedan, and Sister Antoinette from Montreuil. Sister Turgis was to be left at Richelieu. The six others were on their way to serve the sick poor in the hospital at Nantes, in Brittany. After Messieurs the Fathers Administrators, and some of the leading men of the said city, had requested our much honoured Father Monsieur Vincent to send some of his Sisters for this purpose, since they had heard what the Sisters had accomplished in the hospital at Angers, they asked if they might have sent to them a copy of the articles of agreement, and the document for establishing our said Sisters; and they testified that they wished to grant the same terms.

'Our much honoured Father did us the charitable service of giving a conference on the subject, on the previous Monday, upon concluding which he appointed by name the above-mentioned Sisters; and on the Wednesday following I went to receive his instructions for the journey, and had the happiness of receiving his holy blessing; and when I told him of the well-grounded fear that I had, that I should commit many faults on this journey, he of his charity ordered me to write for him a narrative of our doings and encounters during the said journey. Bearing in mind his holy instructions and practices, I formed for myself no other view or intention but that of doing the most holy will of God, and faithfully keeping our rules.

'We were nine in number when we got into the coach for Orleans: that is, the six for Nantes, and the Sister for Richelieu, with Sister Françoise Noret and myself to accompany them. We were very cheerful without, by the grace of God, a failing to observe our rules, except that at the hours of prayer and of silence we allowed ourselves to be overcome by sleep, for which at times we blamed the heat.

'Upon entering the towns and villages, one of us would remember to invoke the Holy Angels, with the prayer that they would take ever more care of the souls in that place, and assist them to glorify God for ever; and on going past the churches, we made acts of adoration of the Most Holy Sacrament, and venerated their holy patrons. Upon arriving at the places where we were to eat or sleep, certain of the Sisters would visit the church to give thanks to God for his protection, to beg him to continue to aid us, that we might have his holy blessing to do his holy will. If there was a hospital, the same Sisters would visit it; if not, they would call on some sick person of the place; and this they did in the name of all our company, to extend the offer of our services and duty to God in the persons of the poor. Whenever we could, we paid a visit to the Church in the mornings before leaving, with the same intentions. Upon occasion, we would speak a few words, either upon those principal points of the faith which it is necessary to know for salvation, or certain little instructions on morals, but briefly.

'After Orleans, we spent a night at Mehun, and because the river was low, we were almost five days on the road after Mehun. We were a night at Cour-sur-Loire, and the next day passed through Monouy, stopping at the port

of Ablevoie, where our dear Sister got down to go to
Richelieu. . . .

'. . . We continued our journey very happily, thank
God, and at Pont-de-Cé we had the honour of being
refused at the inn because we arrived late; but it was
only an excuse because they did not want to kill chickens
for us, and so put us in danger of eating them on Friday;
but after we left that precious house we found a surgeon's
wife who received us kindly.'

The company stopped in Angers to visit the hospital and
the Sisters there. Louise was given a welcome by the civic
authorities and the Ladies of Charity. At Nantes, people were
awaiting their coming with much impatience and a man
was posted to keep an eye on the river so that there should be
no risk of their arrival passing unnoticed. Their disembarka-
tion, before a great concourse of onlookers, was in the nature
of a triumph.

'All the ladies of the town, many in number and high
in rank, took the trouble to come and visit us, and even
those who lived out in the country round about Nantes
made a special journey to see us, so great was their desire
to see our establishment.

'A number of superiors of the reformed orders also
came; and several convents of nuns who could not come
to us insisted that some of the ladies should lead us to
them, which they did, taking along the Sisters one after
the other, for they wanted to see both them and their
habit.'

Once the act of establishment was signed, Louise bade
farewell to the gentlemen, to the Vicar General and to her
dear Sisters and departed, being escorted to the boat by the
same guard of honour. She left the boat at Angers and completed her journey by coach, as contrary winds and water
made river navigation dangerous.

In addition to this narrative which may in a sense be called an official document, Louise mentions in some of her letters particulars of her journey and her stay in Nantes. She affirms with naïve astonishment that she was taken to be a lady of rank. This she certainly was; she bore herself as such and the Marillacs had made so much noise in the world that notice had to be taken of her quality and deportment. She also reported with astonishment and joy that despite the fatigues of the road her health was very good.

> 'My health is so good, that this journey has made me wish I had nothing else to do but run about the country, provided there was something for me to do there.'

Here is an accent which is new: here is the joy of a woman completely mistress of herself, who enjoys good health partly owing to her self-mastery. Louise was now in full control of all her powers and she applied them to the organisation of the Charities. We should take note of the date: it was the year 1645, one of the high points of her life.

The hospital at Nantes was a masterpiece of skill in organisation. Yet the most perfect piece of mechanism will get out of hand and the Nantes system broke down more than once. This is not a history of the foundations of the Daughters of Charity and the story of the house of Nantes would in any case require a volume to itself. The successes of the Daughters were too spectacular and aroused local jealousies; moreover, the Daughters were perhaps a little too conscious of the progress they had made. They were inclined to chatter about it in the town and to encourage the formation of cliques. Harmony among the Daughters themselves was not always complete. The Bishop lent an ear to reports which exaggerated or perverted the truth and began to form a very unfavourable opinion of the Daughters and their work. The 'Fathers of the Poor', jealous of their prerogatives and parsimonious of their funds, came to believe that the Daughters were misusing public money subscribed for the use of the poor. In Paris, Mademoiselle carried the burden of these difficulties, writing by every courier to counsel and to correct. In consultation with Monsieur Vincent, she decided that an official visitation should be made and M. Lambert was sent. Monsieur Vincent himself stayed in Nantes and restored order and peace to the hospital. But he was less successful in dealing with the opposition of the Bishop though he stood up to him firmly in the interests of truth. Louise de Marillac, always pacific by nature, was adamant on one point only: her Daughters had been accused, most odiously and falsely, of pillaging the funds of the poor and of misappropriating hospital equipment. She was disposed to recall the Daughters. She declared with hauteur that once they had shaken the dust of Nantes from their sandals she would be able to say truthfully that they had carried off nothing that belonged to the hospital. When we recall the efforts it had cost the Daughters to clean and equip that ill-found house, we can relish the proud irony of her words. The condition of affairs in Nantes was certainly bad, but in course of time things settled down. The hospital, like other human institutions, continued to have its times of crisis and its times of prosperous tranquillity while, through foul and fair, God and the sick poor were well served by courageous souls.

I have given some particulars of Saint-Germain, Saint-Denis, Angers, Richelieu and Nantes. These foundations were followed by others and the tempo quickened. Wherever the priests planted the Mission, wherever the Ladies of the Hôtel-Dieu had land or interests, the Daughters were wanted. Even the most systematic recruiting was insufficient to meet all the demands.

One of the Ladies of Charity (Marie de Gonzague) became Queen of Poland and wanted to have the Daughters in her country. Hence the daring venture of a foundation in Warsaw—a house whose tribulations were to be a thorny anxiety for Louise. Queen Anne of Austria asked for Daughters to nurse the wounded on the field of battle. So Louise de Marillac's peasant girls, enrolled as servants to carry bowls of soup to the poor, found themselves working as nurses to armies.

The congregation was available for any task of this kind. Its activities were as various as the many faces of human wretchedness. In the course of three centuries they have never ceased to expand and take new forms. Today we may say that no form of human suffering in any country of the world escapes the attention of the Daughters. When they began their work in the rue St Victor, they were five in number; today they are fifty thousand, scattered about the world. And the happy omen of this state of affairs was that consciousness that all was well which filled Louise's spirit during those triumphant days in Nantes.

THORNS AND SMILES

THE MOTHER-HOUSE was now well established in the St Laurent district, opposite the priory and church of St Lazare. The daily routine of this house and of its daughter-houses throughout France was enlivened by many an incident, colourful and gay or sorrowful and moving: small episodes, of little significance in themselves, which stick in the mind and stand out more clearly with the passage of time, like milestones along a road.

Mademoiselle was very reticent about events in her private life and it is only by chance that we come across any information about it.

It was only to be expected that, in the course of her journeys on horseback throughout the Ile de France, Louise should meet a traveller who called a ceremonious greeting as he passed her by; and that she, being a Marillac, should with punctilious correctness acknowledge the courtesy. But the horseman, outwardly so much the gentleman, lacked the gentility to go with the appearance and maliciously spread a tale that Mademoiselle had accepted his offer of marriage. An insignificant and stupid incident, but one which deeply wounded Louise and plunged her into a state of despondency. She sank to a state so low that she had to go for consolation to Monsieur Vincent. But from this she drew a lesson for her community and made it a rule that Sisters travelling on the public roads should hold no speech with men.

Calumny may be a source of sorrow. At Liancourt certain scatter-brained young people spread a story that the Daughters were flighty and had joined them in doubtful recreations. The slander gathered substance as it passed from mouth to mouth, though Sister Mathurine Guérin's bearing was well above suspicion. The Superior of the Nicolaïtes, the parish curate, a severe man tinged with Jansenism, interrogated the young accusers. They stuck to their story, though they brought no evidence, and the priest believed it. The Sisters were refused absolution and excluded from communion. They bore their sentence with humility and in silence, although they suffered painfully. There was a great scandal and many lies were accepted as truth. Inevitably the facts of the case were at length discovered. The accusers withdrew their lie, the Daughters were cleared of blame. They had done no wrong and so had suffered no loss. The trial had been a source of spiritual progress to them.

At Char the suffering was not of this dramatic character. Rather it was a long drawn out battle between the Jansenist curate and the Daughters, who did not understand Jansenism, but suffered because of it. Louise was most vigilant on this point and protected her Daughters from Jansenist contagion, just as carefully as Monsieur Vincent guarded the Priests of the Mission. She had her theological arguments for she knew her theology. But she also had her practical reasons: if her Daughters were to fill their heads with doctrine which they did not understand, they would no longer have the heart for their humble work. They were called to serve the sick and not to discourse upon theology.

Louise had lifted her girls from ignorance; she had taught them to read and write so that they could share their lives with her when they were away. What more natural than that one of her Daughters, proud of knowing how to write and eager to show off her skill, should carry on a secret correspondence with a village friend? This could lead to mischief if it were not guarded against. There is a protection in the simplicity of ignorance.

Another of the girls had her head turned by the novel responsibilities of her nursing career. She learnt in secret the art of drawing blood, received from a proud mother the gift of a lancet and proceeded to bleed her patients indiscriminately and quite without method or authority. When another

Sister endeavoured to confiscate the forbidden lancet, the
rebellious Daughter refused to give it up. She declared that
she had thrown it away with the dressing to deliver herself
from temptation.

It was hard to know what to do with cases such as these.
Monsieur Vincent counselled moderation; the devil would
grow weary of tempting, heads would cool, grace would
flow again in torrents. There were times when nothing could
be done and then the girl had to leave. Perhaps there were
faults on both sides, but a girl who had mistaken her
vocation had to go back into the world. Occasionally her
exodus was coloured by a touch of the picturesque. One of
the girls who left the community carried away with her some
of the poultry, and Mademoiselle had no reason to doubt
that the culprit sold them for good money. Another went
even further, for she took the money-box. This girl had been
chosen, in answer to an appeal from Alain de Solminhac, to
go to Cahors to manage an orphanage. Off she went, well
supplied with money for her needs upon the road and with
something over. She disappeared into the world without a
sound, and Alain de Solminhac and his orphanage waited
for two years—for a Daughter who was never heard of again.
This was a serious matter, for the missing money had been
provided by the Bishop of Cahors who was thus let down
twice over.

These, however, were only small events in the life of a new
community which was still defining its aims and finding its
equilibrium. The greatest trial of all was inescapable: deaths
occurred very frequently among the Daughters, for in the
early years of enthusiasm the generous girls expended their
strength without stint and died of exhaustion. Louise was
always heart-broken; she held herself responsible for the
deaths of her Daughters—she had not watched over them
with sufficient care and God was punishing her for her sins
by striking down those she held most dear.

In a way she felt constant dread on this score. She was

always anxious for the girls, especially if they were in places where the plague was raging and nothing could protect them from contagion. She took the trouble to send to Sister Jeanne Lepeintre, at Angers, a box of some popular remedy which if carefully used would, so people said, give complete protection from the plague. All her Daughters were carried in her heart. She suffered whenever she thought that any one of them was aggrieved or disturbed. The Daughters at Ussel thought that life in their mountain solitude was something of a penance; they complained of 'that wretched Louise', and sometimes they grizzled outright. But Mademoiselle had no time for grizzlers. A Daughter of Charity should be gay and cheerful and not a grizzler.

At the mother-house, gaiety was the rule. There were always some girls who had their heads in the air and occasionally lost their tempers, especially when they had to take their turn of duty in the water-queue. The house had no well and the community was too poor to buy from the water merchant, so the girls had to take their turn at the public fountain, wait in the queue for it to open, and stand patiently among housewives who exchanged doubtful stories and poked fun at the Daughters. It happened one day that a Daughter on duty at the fountain was fed up, turned her back on the fountain, and carried her buckets to the door of the house at St Lazare, where there was a well, and asked the Brothers to draw water for her. To her confusion, it was not a Brother, but Monsieur Vincent himself who filled the buckets for her and carried them back to the door of the Daughters' house. Mademoiselle at once decided that she must have her own well and a well she got.

There were in these unlettered girls great treasures of delicacy and feeling. These would come to light in quite unexpected ways, and Mademoiselle would be enchanted. She wrote:

'I have been much consoled to learn that a poor patient has had a fight with one of our Sisters who, by the grace

of God, did nothing to defend herself. The man was a
little rough with his instruction. We are servants of the
poor, and therefore we have to suffer such correction.'
We may almost glimpse the smile with which she told the
story.

One Sister submits to attack from the poor fellow she is
nursing; others decline to wait upon the rich. The duchesse
d'Aiguillon, Queen Marie de Gonzague of Poland and the
Queen of Austria herself, struck by the demeanour of the
Daughters of Charity, all cherished hopes of having one or
two of the girls as members of their own households. It was
not easy to refuse the requests of ladies of rank so eminent as
these, especially as they were people who truly loved the
company and gave it valuable support. But Monsieur Vincent
marvelled at the reply which was transmitted by the
Daughters:

'Yesterday, being pressed by Mme de Combalet to
send her one of the girls for her own service, I mentioned
it to Marie Denyse, as she seemed to me the most suitable
girl to send; but she made me an answer worthy of a girl
whose vocation is to God and to charity, which was, that
she had left mother and father to give herself to the
service of the poor for the love of God, and begged to be
excused if she could not change this intention to go and
serve this great lady. After that, I spoke to big Barbara,
without saying who it was for, or why, and sent her to
wait for me at the house of the said Mme de Combalet,
where I said that this good lady would employ her, partly
in her own service and partly for the poor of that parish.
She began to cry, but when she gave her consent, I
handed her over to a maid of the said lady. But I was
much astonished when, immediately after that, having
gone to pay a call on the Abbé de Loyac, Barbara came
to me there. She said she was dumb-founded to see such
grand company, she could not possibly live there, she
begged me to take her back. Our Lord had given her to

the poor, would I not send her back to them? Which
much astonished the Abbé, to see such a scorn for the
glories of the world, so that he made me tell the good girl
to go back to the said lady; and if after four or five days
she still found she was not happy, then she should return
to Saint-Nicholas. What do you think of that, Mademoiselle? Are you not enraptured to see the strength of the
Spirit of God in these two poor girls, and the contempt
he makes them feel for the world and its glories?'

The same thing happened when the Queen of Poland and
the Queen of France asked for girls for their households.
Decidedly the spirit of the company was by this time firmly
founded: there were the poor, and after them—nobody.

We now come to the Vigil of Pentecost, (always a day of
importance in the life of Louise de Marillac) the Vigil of
Pentecost 1644. On this day, there occurred in the mother-
house an event which came near to ending in catastrophe.
Louise described it briefly in a letter to Sister Claude at
Angers:

'Oh do all of you, my dear sisters, give hearty
thanks to God for his mercy towards us in saving us
from death on the Vigil of Pentecost, when the floor of
our room collapsed, and we had no more warning than
sufficed to step back about four paces.'

On the anniversary of that day in 1645, in a conference
given in that same room, Monsieur Vincent gives a few more
details:

'Do you think that this floor beneath us, which fell in
a year ago, is a poor proof [of the providence of God]?
A proof it certainly is! That a great beam should give
way in a place like this, and nobody be standing above
or below it—that is miraculous. Mademoiselle Le Gras
was there; a Sister heard the cracking and said the room
was not safe. Mademoiselle made nothing of it. But a
senior Sister repeated the warning. Mademoiselle
deferred to her age, and left the room. She was scarcely

in the next apartment—you can see for yourselves,
Sisters: it is but three paces—when the beam broke and
the floor fell in. Did that happen without the special
providence of God? That very afternoon, I myself ought
to have been here; we were to have met in committee on
some important business. In the noise that there is in a
meeting, nobody would have heard the cracking of that
beam. That Sister would not have been present, for the
Sisters do not come to such meetings, and we should all
have been crushed down there; but God caused some
affair to come along which kept me away from the
meeting, and which meant that none of the Ladies would
be there.

'That was not a matter of mere chance, my Daughters.
We must be very careful not to believe that.'

This accident, which was happily not serious, impressed
Louise de Marillac to quite an extraordinary degree. Her
devotion was always particularly warm at the season of
Pentecost and she was very open to the influences of the Holy
Spirit. She saw in the mishap a very special sign that her
congregation was under the protection of Providence. She
saw it as an intimation from God to make an end of the
anxieties she still held for the future of her work, which was
so manifestly the work of God. Pentecost 1644 became a
landmark in her life. It was as though she had reached the
summit of a mountain, and below her the whole world spread
out in the light of a new day.

She felt this again strongly at Nantes (for this was the
year of that epoch-making journey). She felt it in both mind
and body, as she regained mastery over both. This too was a
providential development, for Monsieur Vincent, already
absorbed in his burden of work for the Mission, was obliged
to collaborate with the Queen in affairs of state, so far as
they bore upon Church affairs; heavily burdened by his work
for the Church, all but overwhelmed by his duties as a
political adviser, he could not devote his time to Mademoiselle

as he had done hitherto. We observe that he begins to answer
her letters with a 'yes' or a 'no', written in the margins of the
letters themselves.

Thus Louise now had to manage not only her house but
herself. She was ready for both tasks. We shall see later that
this date was equally significant for her interior life. From
now on began in her a transformation which rapidly
developed as she made strides towards sanctity. Pentecost
1644 corresponded to the unforgettable Pentecost of 1623
and the two dates became as it were the hinges of her life.

For the moment her earthly home lay in ruins and had to
be repaired. Here her practical genius worked wonders. She
knew the price of materials, knew what it cost, for example,
to weave an ell of serge for a Sister's habit and how much
cheaper it was to get it made in the country. She knew the
wage of a mason's labourer and what food she would have
to provide if she offered to board him. She was not unaware
that prices had risen since her youth and that (as though by
law) in Paris prices double every fifty years. The magnificent
project laid before her by her architect did not, therefore,
take her unawares, and with a very firm courtesy she cut his
plans by half:

'Monsieur,
    'The perfect confidence that I have, that you will have
the goodness to take notice of the request I made to you
about our little plans, makes me recall to your memory
that it is absolutely necessary that the house should be
such as to please my country girls, and that it should be as
far as possible from looking magnificent. I know that
you will not be able to bring yourself down to this level
without some difficulty, because of your habit of designing
everything large and high, but after you have reflected
upon what I have said to you on the subject, and on the
need of the Company to appear in all things poor and
humble if it is to endure, you will clearly see, Monsieur,

that it is a work for our Lord, and it may be that you will be very pleased to contribute to the solidity of the house by means of the gifts that God has given to you, telling you also that all that part which at St Laurent we call the parlour and the kitchen, is also all the room we have for our school and also for bandaging and bleeding the poor.'

The practical good sense of the foundress was, as always, in accord with the principles of Christian perfection and with the spirit of the community. I might have ventured the remark that this harmony was to be found in all her dealings throughout her life, were it not that such an assertion smacks a little of hagiography. It seems to me that in Louise de Marillac, harmony was sometimes shattered by a too professional attitude to her work.

Mademoiselle's attitude to life was that of a sick-nurse. She was always preoccupied with the care of the sick and was forever in quest of new remedies—remedies that would cure. She was very much in agreement on this point with Madame Fouquet, who had even compiled a book on home nursing and popular medicine. She was still more in accord with Monsieur Vincent, who likewise appears to have been at times an enthusiast for strange cures. Their letters to one another on the subject are most revealing. Here we have two active temperaments entirely absorbed in what they are doing and each of them constantly held back by ill-health— Monsieur Vincent by fevers and ague, and Mademoiselle by disorders of the stomach. As their medicines never cured them, they were always in quest of new ones and both lent a ready ear to those vendors of patent medicines so numerous in every age. Mademoiselle declared that Monsieur Vincent was not taking due care; the priest said that Louise was neglecting her health and overtiring her strength. There is in this correspondence something like an obsession with illness, with a vast amount of detail on remedies and their physiological effects, which reminds us of Molière's *Le Malade*

Imaginaire. It borders on the absurd when Mademoiselle, prescribing for Monsieur Vincent's leg wound, orders a course of purges and blood-letting, or a syrup of peach flowers which is said to work wonders. There is enough material in this body of letters to provide a substantial treatise on the official and popular medicine of the day. Both had their laughable side and occasionally, like the quacks of today, they could claim a cure. Despite the not infrequent setbacks, Mademoiselle believed firmly in her own methods —so firmly that she can perhaps be charged with superstition in matters medical. Yet it may well be that a certain appeal to superstition was in those days necessary to keep up the morale of the sick—and that too was an aspect of charity.

There is one domain, brimfull with sadness, in which despite all her efforts Louise never achieved serenity and equilibrium. She was, if possible, more completely a mother than other mothers and Monsieur Vincent says of her that her maternal feelings over-flowed the measure but were ever shot through with fear and impatience. Her son Michel was backward and unstable from birth. He developed slowly under his mother's anxious eye. When the boy was thirteen years old and his mother began to travel, she placed him as a boarder in the seminary for young clerics conducted by M. Bourdoise at Saint-Nicholas-du-Chardonnet. Life as an intern in this little suburban school was very hard for the moody boy even though Monsieur Vincent, almost his neighbour at the Collège des Bons Enfants, gave him a home in his holidays. The break in the school routine only gave the fond mother an opportunity to coddle the lad with blood-lettings and purges in an effort to improve his condition.

Louise de Marillac had dreamed and made up her mind that her son should be a priest. He was therefore clad in the soutane at the earliest possible age, removed from the college at Saint-Nicolas and entered at the Collège de Clermont, where he was to continue his studies by reading theology with the Jesuits. In the letters which passed between his mother and Monsieur Vincent we follow the history of Michel's health, his studies, his whims, his dislikes, his good resolutions, his purges and bleedings, his tempers and repentances. He was a child like other children, sometimes delightful, not knowing what he wanted to do and as often as not content to do nothing. His mother supposed that all he needed was a spur and so she gave him incentives in plenty, especially when the time came for him to decide whether to take minor orders. At this point we share in a drama of passion, of conflicting desires. Monsieur Vincent endeavoured to soothe both mother and son and from his letters we get an idea of the strong feeling on both sides:

To Louise De Marillac.

Saturday morning.

'I received your letter this morning, and write at once in reply to tell you what your son has been saying to M. de la Salle. He says he is only entering into this state because such is your desire; that his desire is to be dead* therefore, but that to please you he would take minor orders. Now, is that a vocation? I think he would prefer to die himself than that you should do so. However that may be, and whether it springs from [human] nature or from the devil, his will is not at present free. He is not able to reach his own decision, and that in a matter of the greatest importance. You would surely not desire that? Not long ago, there was a good lad in this town who took the sub-diaconate in just the same circumstances, and then could not pass to the higher orders. Would you wish to expose your son to a danger like that? Leave him to the guidance of God who is much more his Father than you are his mother, and loves him more than you can do. Let God have the guidance of your son. He will know how to call him at another time, if he so desires, or to give him some

---

* Monsieur Vincent had first written, and then erased: 'that he wished you were dead, and himself too'.

occupation suitable to his health. I recall a certain priest who used to be here in this house, who came to his priesthood in just such trouble of mind—and God knows what has become of him now. . . .'

V.D.

I request you to make your meditation on the mother of Zebedee's children: to whom, when she was over-eager for the position of her sons, our Saviour said: 'You know not what you ask'. (*vide* Matt. xx, 20.)

To Louise de Marillac.

'I have received two letters from you, or, more correctly, one letter in two parts, and have since seen and spoken to your son, without letting him know that I had any knowledge of what passed yesterday; now, he tells me in a very recollected and tranquil way that he has seen you and that you had a little difference of opinion. Then I spoke to him of his vocation, and asked if he was going to persevere in it. Then he told me with much good will that he would, and that he was going to the Sorbonne with this intention, determined to do well. This makes me think that there was no need for me to speak to him and that we need not disturb him in that matter about which you are anxious. I therefore beg you to be at peace; and what is more, if the things you dread should happen, it would still be needful to adore the Providence of God concerning him, and to believe that travel, or a change of condition, would be good for his health, and perhaps contribute to a greater degree of perfection. Alas, Mademoiselle, if all those who had put a distance between themselves and their parents had put their souls in danger, where should I be? Well, remember that all things serve the predestined to bring them to their goal, and that I am, Mademoiselle, in the love of our Saviour, your very humble servant,

VINCENT DEPAUL.'

A boy who desires the death of his mother, and of himself; a mother and son who engage in argument, and say things so hard that the mother loses her gift of understanding—here is a situation which throws some light on the soul of Louise and the emotions that control it. She smothered her emotions: necessity had long ago taught her how to; but sometimes nature gained the upper hand. She reproached herself for giving way to natural feeling and made scruples of her faults. She endeavoured to detach herself from Michel and for the future to look on him only as a child of God.

These events were taking place at a time (1644) when a new political climate began to be noticeable in France, infecting to some extent the revived spiritual life of the nation. But the ground lost was quickly regained. Paul de Gondi was appointed coadjutor to the Archbishop of Paris, and it was remembered that Vincent de Paul had a point of contact with the Gondi family. The support of Paul de Gondi was therefore solicited with a view to obtaining for the young cleric a post in the household of the future Cardinal-Bishop. Louise made no direct approach but was willing that overtures should be made on her behalf. Then she reproached herself for the liveliness of her own hopes and passed through torments as the affair made its slow progress. In the end the plan fell through and Michel renounced his intention to enter the Church.

He escaped from seminary discipline and for some time lived as do other young men, without very much in the way of grave fault. His mother made too much of his misdemeanours, grieved over them—and persuaded herself that he was no longer her responsibility. Monsieur Vincent appointed him a bailiff at Saint-Lazare and there was some talk of getting him married. Maternal feeling at once revived in the bosom of Louise and her heart was plunged into tumult over her son's marriage.

The marriage contract was a difficult matter. Michel was without fortune and his post as bailiff at Saint-Lazare carried no salary. The uncle of his intended bride, Réné Michel de la Rochemaillet, agreed to cede to Michel Le Gras his post of solicitor to the Mint; but for this money was required—and there was no money. It occurred to Louise that Monsieur Vincent could petition the Queen, or that something could be requested of the d'Attichy family, who owed a good deal to the de Gras family. In the end, everything was settled. The marriage contract was signed in the presence of Monsieur Vincent. The marriage of Michel Le Gras and Gabrielle Le Clerc de Chênevière was celebrated in the Eglise Saint-Sauveur on January 18th, 1650. The sky cleared at last and in due course there arrived another Louise, who was much fêted in the community as 'the little Sister'. It is said, however, that Michel was a trial to his mother to the end of her life. There were wrangles and quarrels in the wife's family and Louise had to be brought in as peacemaker. Then Michel became deaf and had to give up his office as solicitor to the Mint.

Louise carried to the grave her anxiety for her son. She had always harboured a vague notion that this boy had been sent to her as a punishment: she despised this thought and overcame it by her confidence in the goodness of God; but she could not help suffering and used to say that since her birth not a single day of her life had passed without sorrow.

It is only the mediocre soul which never suffers.

PART III

GREAT CONCERNS

A SPIRITUAL TRAINING

WHILE Louise de Marillac was mastering as well as she could the troubles of her soul, presiding over her foundations and governing her houses, the heavy anxieties which all this work involved absorbed her thoughts and exhausted her strength.

One of her responsibilities was the spiritual training of her Daughters. At first the work had been pressed forward with all urgency and Louise had been content to make of her girls exemplary Christians and highly efficient nurses. But Mademoiselle was far-sighted: she regarded it as part of her vocation to lead her Christian girls farther forward into the love of God, a road along which they could travel a great distance.

She would have to begin quietly with the human virtues, which would serve to sustain the supernatural virtues and those virtues of vocation which are most pleasing to God. This was the work which Louise de Marillac proposed to herself.

Her Daughters were ever present to her heart. Since each one of them had passed through her own hands, she knew their souls as well as she knew their faces; and as she had visited many of the places whence the girls came or where they were working, she could set each girl, not only in one of the houses of the community, but in a spiritual homeland. They lived in communities of two or three or more. If any one of them should ever have to work alone it would be for a time only, and Mademoiselle would suffer in sympathy the effects of that solitude, well knowing from experience that loneliness is a promoter of sadness.

The community day began at four in the morning. In Angers, in Nantes, at Saint-Denis, at Saint-Germain, at

Richelieu and elsewhere the bell would ring and its summons would be disputed by none. The first two hours of the day, as was formally stipulated in the contract, belonged exclusively to the Sisters for their private, secret life with God, except when a patient in danger required their instant help. Through every hour of the day, the details of the Rule continued to protect them and to keep them for God. But the Rule was relaxed for the sick; everything, Jesus Christ himself, was to be left that he might be served in his suffering members and be re-discovered in them.

The Daughters did not belong to themselves but to the poor and the sick, their true masters.

To the service of their patients they were to apply themselves with sweetness and respectful courtesy. Not a single letter did Louise write to them without a reminder of this fundamental law of their calling. They were the servants of the sick and the poor. The term 'Daughter' in the language of the time signified 'servant', and the community had taken the name because of this meaning. This was a great feature of their life in the eyes of the world and they must be penetrated with it from the first moment of the day.

These masters, the sick poor, were difficult at times, because they were suffering. The girls must love them greatly to bear with them. To stoop to this humility, they must first stoop to bearing with their own companions: they had to live with each other, day and night, through all the hours that came, even when they were not in sight. This was difficult, as Louise well knew, and she never wearied of reminding her Daughters that without mutual forbearance life in community can be torment, when it should be a paradise.

On one occasion she wrote to the Sisters at Bernay:

'It seems to me that I can see both of you in a state of great peace, and with a desire to arouse in yourselves a longing for unity and cordiality. This would consist in your giving yourselves to each other, telling one another

what you have done while you were apart, telling one
another also where you are going when you go out; the
one out of an obligation to humility and the other by an
obligation of mutual support and confidence. Similarly,
in your little exercises: if one be sad, let her master her
sadness to take recreation with her sister; and let her
who is joyful moderate her happiness to suit the mood of
the other, and so, little by little, to draw her out of her
melancholy; all this for the love of our Lord and so that
you will not listen to any temptation which might cause
you to desire to go elsewhere, looking for satisfaction and
relief for your own poor heart: that would be the total
ruin of that holy friendship in which two Sisters should
live together, in which I beg our Lord to preserve you in
his holy love; in which I am . . .'

Bearing with one another and bearing each her share of
the common misery, the girls must recognise that they each
had shoulders and a heart fit for the burden:

'All the afflictions and losses which happened at
Angers caused me extreme suffering for the trials which
the poor of that place had to endure; I beg the Divine
Goodness to comfort them and to give them the assistance
that they need. My very dear Sisters, you have been in
very great troubles; but have you well considered that it
was just that the servants of the poor should suffer with
their Master, and that each of us deserves to bear in her
own body her share of those scourges which God sends
upon mankind at large? Oh, my dear Sisters, how often
are we obliged to make this meditation: "Who are we,
that we should have received one of the greatest graces
that God can bestow on any creature of any condition,
in calling us into his service? And would we wish to be
exempt from all discomfort?" Oh, my dear Sisters, let us
protect ourselves carefully against such a thought; but
rather let us very often be astonished, that God should
have removed us from places where we might, in the

company of the world, have suffered much; and that he
should have given us bread, and put us so much at our
ease, and caused us to dwell in safety. My dear Sisters,
how heavy is the obligation thus laid upon us to habits of
virtue, if we are not to pay dearly for it in the next world!
Let us not wait for that penalty, but let us do whatever
we can to acquire the virtues God asks of us, in thanks-
giving for the graces he bestows on us every day. I do
not know, my dear Sisters, whether you ever received a
letter in which I discoursed to you on this subject.

'In the name of God, take good care, I beg you, to be
lovers of the sturdy virtues, particularly of humility and
patience. If I speak to you often on the subject, it is
because for some time now I have been receiving
intimations that it is necessary for me to do so. Also, the
Ladies who come visiting expect to be given some kind
of welcome. You know, my Sister, how our Sisters who
make ready the dinners take care that all should be
satisfied. It is true that your other duties in the service
of the sick take up all your time. But when the Ladies
come, you may hand over your duties to another Sister,
sometimes one, and sometimes another, so as to give them
the best satisfaction you can without going against the
orders of the Fathers. A good understanding between
yourselves will accomplish all things.

'In God's name, Sister Cecilia, raise yourself just a little
above your small distastes, and hope to be given opportunities for obedience, not with a hope which makes you
anxious, but patient and peaceful; and do unto others as
you would wish them to do unto you. Above all, be very
compliant, and welcome pleasantly those—if there be
any such—who may find it a thankless task to put up
with you. Commend me well to all our Sisters, whom I
embrace with all my heart. To them, as to you, I am, in
the love of Jesus Crucified . . .'

It happened occasionally that the tares of discord sprang

up among the Sisters and Mademoiselle would then adopt
a tone of severe reproach, softened only by distance. Sisters
Barbara and Louise at Richelieu had to suffer the sharp
edge of her tongue:

'I have learned, as I always feared I might, that your
little occupations, which were succeeding so well for the
consolation of the sick and the teaching of little girls, have
contributed nothing to your own perfection; on the
contrary, it appears to have done you harm, since the
good odour that used to come from you begins to be lost.
Think, my dear Sisters, what you are doing: you are a
cause why God is offended in a place where he used to be
glorified, your neighbour takes scandal, and you give
people cause not to prize as highly as they should the holy
exercise of charity. How will you dare one day to appear
before God, to give an account of the use you have made
of his great grace in calling you to the state in which he
has put you? He expected to derive from it his own glory,
and behold, you are the usurper, you, Sister Barbara, by
your lack of cordiality towards the Sister God has given
you, by your little actions of contempt, and your small
negligences, and by your small forbearance with her
infirmities. How is it that you can never bear in mind,
that when you were put with her to be to her in the
position of a Superior, this laid on you the duties of a
mother, but heavier than the duties of a mother in the
flesh; for you were to make more effort for her salvation
and her perfection than earthly mothers commonly do,
and this obliged you to exercise great patience and
charity, as the Son of God commanded when he walked
the earth. And having accepted this responsibility, did
you not at once perceive what a degree of humility it
would require, since you have so much reason to know
your own incapacity? Ought you not always to have
before your eyes, when you give any command, that it is
obedience which causes you to give that order, and not

that of your self you would have any right to do it? Now,
my dear Sister, I hope that the harm is not yet so far gone
that it cannot be remedied. Set your own faults firmly
before your own eyes, without excusing yourself, for
indeed nothing can be the cause of any evil that we do,
but we ourselves. Acknowledge this truth before God, stir
up in your heart a great love for our dear Sister Louise,
and in the sight of the merciful justice of the good God,
throw yourself at her feet, and beg pardon of her for your
lack of cordiality to her, and for all the sorrows you have
caused her; with the promise that, by the grace of God,
you will love her as Jesus Christ himself loves her; take
all the care of her you ought to take, and embrace her,
having this true feeling for her in your heart.

'And you, my dear Sister Louise, here you are again,
falling into your little bad habits. What do you think of
your state? Is yours a life of liberty? Very far from it.
Your life should be one long act of humility and obedience. Is it possible that you never think of that? Or is it
that, if you do think of it, you have so little love of God,
and so little fear for your own salvation, that you neglect
those things to which you are bound? My Daughter, do
yourself a little violence. What comes over you, when you
pay calls or go on pilgrimage without permission, so
that you apparently desire to live in all things according
to your own will? Do you never remember that you
should do nothing, nor go anywhere, without the permission of Sister Barbara, whom you accepted as your
Superior before you went away, and whom you ought to
love as much as, or more than, you would your own
mother? I declare you never seem to recall to mind what
is your state, since you do so many things incompatible
with it. Would you not be sorry if you lost your state for
such poor satisfactions? I believe that the cause of most
of your faults is that you have money, and have always
been pleased to have it. If you will believe me, you will

rid yourself of this affection. Put it all into the hands of
Sister Barbara; only desire to have what she thinks right,
and stir yourself up to love poverty, in honour of that of
the Son of God. By this means you will attain what is
necessary to be truly a Daughter of Charity.'

This long letter, so firm and to the point, is that of the head
of a community and of a mother.

Her liveliest expressions of reproach are never bitter.
Sometimes they take on inflexions of tenderness. It is certainly
tenderness which is most apparent in her teaching—a very
anxious tenderness when the health of any of her Daughters
is in danger; a tenderness skilful and delicate on those many
occasions when consolation was required. The imagination
of a Sister may have been too active: clouds have gathered,
such as we call scruples. These scruples play a large part in
the interior life, especially in those cases where self-examination is carried too far. This leads to disgust with the basic
virtues, and a search for imaginary virtues creating anxieties
that are not grounded in reason.

Louise writes to a Sister:

'I will try to help you to get rid of your scruples, having
suffered from the same ones myself. Try to dissolve them
in other interests, instead of struggling with them directly,
and ask the Holy Spirit to give you joy.'

It is by her tenderness that she consoles, but it is an
affection which has about it something virile. She drew great
distinction between the tenderness which is the strength and
depth of charity and that softness which is a serious defect.
The latter is a kind of immature delicacy, which is upset by
the slightest breath and creates for itself the most extraordinary scruples. A person may form a dislike for going to a
particular confessor, or he may scruple because he is too
much inclined to go to another. Sooner or later he must rid
himself of this kind of softness. 'Our much honoured Father',
she said, 'told us in his last conference that we must detach
ourselves from these levities, which are much more dangerous

in us than in nuns, because we never have the time to reflect
on ourselves; our patients claim us.'

Where a sharper reproach was necessary Louise did not
hesitate to come straight to the point; but she believed that
the lesson would be more effective if it came from a higher
authority. On these occasions she invited Monsieur Vincent,
or M. de Vaux, or M. Portail, to be the correcting Father,
and while she apologised for her own boldness, she told them
plainly what they should know and what she wanted them to
say:

'Take note, Monsieur, if you please, that it was Sister
Anne rather than Sister Marguerite who introduced the
style of arranging the hair, about which you did me the
honour to ask; for I know that she tends very strongly to
set herself up for a person of much experience, a woman
very devout and very wise, not to say full of self-conceit,
and is so, everywhere, as much with the Ladies as with
the poor, and she loves to say a great deal about humility,
but this is a form of self-praise. There is a great deal
wrong; but I only mean to speak, Monsieur, of her
natural dispositions, and hope that grace may draw some
good out of them.'

It is the function of a head to make reason prevail; but it
is the heart which is in control; and reason and the heart are
both in the hands of God. Consolation, counsel or reproach,
all lead back to the centre which is the love of God.

In every word of every letter from the Foundress love flows
like an impalpable grace, not only in formulas convention-
ally used, which despite the convention never lack sincerity,
but also in the substance of what she says and her tone of
voice heard at a distance by all her Sisters. The formation
that she gave, into which she put so much tenderness, was
never in the least mawkish or pointless or petty. Many little
things had to be said, but once said a few words brought her
hearers back to the true framework of her teaching, which is
noble and serious. She could abruptly bring to end a letter

full of the most detailed advice, on a note that is very modern: 'Let us pray, my Daughters, for France and for the Church'.

These were the sinister years of the Fronde, of princes who exploited to the full the wretchedness and anger of the people and made the young king pay dearly for the violence of the minister who had laid the foundations of his reign. Louise de Marillac had suffered from the excesses of that violence and now she could feel how full of peril were the forces of reaction not only for the king, but for the nation itself and therefore for the Church. Her anxieties and her prayers joined with those of Vincent de Paul and she endeavoured to unite with her own the intentions of her Daughters. Those poor girls from the fields, through close acquaintance with human misery, had grown capable of entering into the real needs of Christianity and the state. The Daughters were in no peril of losing themselves in the great questions of policy, which there was no need for them to understand; for a single principle, which was the very clear expression of a love made to their measure, dominated their lives: the principle of 'holy indifference', or of total submission to the Divine Will.

Correspondence going into great detail and rising to lofty heights was the great instrument used by Louise for the formation of her girls. A letter written by her is a continuous conversation, a conference always returning to the main points. In our day, we have given to this word 'conference' a solemn meaning of diplomatic negotiation or learned discussion. In fact, a conference is no more than an orderly conversation and he who directs it gives it his own character. It was thus that Louise de Marillac understood the word when she conferred with her Daughters; and thus Vincent de Paul understood it when he came to speak of God and to define in the presence of God the spirit that should animate a true Daughter of Charity.

At these celebrated conferences, given once or twice each month, everyone was present. Daughters who were serving Charities in the parishes and who were not detained by urgent services to the sick joined the Daughters of the mother-house. The subject of the conference had been announced by letter, and in the course of the week or fortnight each girl had meditated and reasoned, with all the ability which God had planted beneath her hood. Shy girls had permission to write down their contribution and to bring their paper to the meeting. Every girl could speak, and she would be interrogated, not as a child at a school examination, but as a member of the community with a contribution to make to the common spiritual treasury.

Monsieur Vincent had made his meditation on the theme. Mademoiselle, with much humility and plain goodness, excusing her own boldness, turned her reflections in the direction of her Daughters' needs which she very well understood. With a familiarity which reassured the most timid, the much-honoured Father would begin by bringing forward the youngest and least fluent among the girls. On getting an answer full of good sense, he would cry out with sincere admiration for he could always perceive behind the simplest words the most profound reality. In turning it over and repeating it and adding appropriate words of his own, he would throw the subject into relief: the pebble picked up on the road became a diamond, and the astonished little Sister could well believe that God had given her thoughts both rich and beautiful. Monsieur Vincent would then bring forward the more senior Sisters and finally, with much respect, Mademoiselle. Then Monsieur Vincent would conclude by summing up. He himself always took the trouble to make notes of his own 'little thoughts', as he called them; and Mademoiselle contrived very skilfully that he should always leave these notes behind. After he had gone the best heads in the house would bend over them. Minutes would be made, a record sincere and complete of every accent and incident, every word spoken; preserving, too, every word of the much-honoured Father, with all his brusqueness, his picturesque turns of phrase and his warmth. The Daughters of Charity are accustomed, and with good reason, to regard the records of these conferences as the charter of their institute.

No attempt has ever been made to define the respective shares of Founder and Foundress in the formal instruction given to the Sisters. This discretion we shall respect and imitate.

On one point we must express regret. Transcripts were made of these conference notes for circulation to the various houses of the Institute. A deplorable custom grew up of introducing various modifications into the text, apparently with a view to bringing the language up to date. Thus the native sharpness has been refined and polished to vanishing point; long passages have been abridged; short and pithy paragraphs have been amplified. Yet, despite this shocking custom, which to this day has not entirely disappeared, the texts of the conferences still bear a stamp of authenticity. As we read them we feel that we are in touch with the minds of the Founders; we almost imagine that we see and hear them, so living and so strong is their thought, even within the conventional formulas of instruction.

Many of the conference notes have completely disappeared with the passage of the years. Those which survive in the edition of Pierre Coste* form a collection of the greatest spiritual value. Taken with the letters written by Mademoiselle, they hold all the instruction received by a Daughter of Charity.

The subjects dealt with are, as a rule, the same as those of the conferences given to the Ladies of Charity, the Daughters of Mary of the Visitation, and the clergy at Saint-Lazare: the love of God and our neighbour, which contains the whole of the Christian law, but with special application to the particular vocation of the Daughters.

---

* This could be called the Critical Edition, had not the editor himself been guilty of making amendments of his own to the original text, no doubt for the best of reasons. (*Author*).

Minute attention is given to the definition of this vocation, its
spirit and its dignity.

The girls are to be the servants of the poor of Jesus Christ;
all the ordinary obligations of Christianity are interpreted
to them in the light of this principle and are repeatedly
brought back to it. Charity to one's neighbour necessarily
begins in love of one's own Sister, in mutual help and forbearance, in affectionate understanding and agreement.
Without these things, the community would be bound to
break up and perish.

Feeling in the meeting would at times run so strong on
this point that an interval had to be allowed for scenes of
reconciliation and pardon, with smiles and tears and
embraces. The grounds of the dispute had been childish and
silly: but it is the tapered dagger which makes the deepest
wound. Happy the wounds which give occasion for heroic
pardon and reparation without measure. Fraternal charity
is a somewhat delicate virtue, inevitably injured by com-
placency, self-confidence or pride. We know from a text
already cited how firmly Monsieur Vincent insisted on that
simplicity which he so admired in 'village girls', provided
they were unspoiled by any subtle contagion from the city,
such as sometimes gets into country air.

The discourse would often deal with another virtue,
regarded by Founder and Foundress as of fundamental
importance. This was the virtue of 'holy indifference'.
Saint Vincent teaches that to be 'indifferent' is to desire
nothing, to ask for nothing, to refuse nothing; to be attached
to no duty, no place, no person; to be ready always either
to depart or to stay, to undertake all things or to leave all
things in obedience to the will of a superior, which is to say,
to the will of God. This subject is discussed in every possible
context, illuminated by psychological penetrations of great
subtlety. The audience can never have wearied during these
conferences at the mother house, as Monsieur Vincent told
his stories punctuated with vigorous action. He had a

large repertoire of anecdote which he loved to emphasise
with telling gesture:

'I once knew a good lady who loved nothing in the
world but her dog—and how she loved it! One day, as
they were going on a journey, the dog died. What
lamentations she raised, because she had lost her dog!
'Who will come to meet me now', she cried, 'when I get
back home? For my dog, my consolation and amusement, is dead!' Poor creature! She sighed as she sat in her
carriage—and why? For a dog. She was so much upset
that she thought she was going out of her senses, and the
doctors advised her to do a little travelling to distract her
mind. Oh, my Daughters! If love for a wretched animal
could have an effect like that . . .!'

One of the Sisters remarked that the only means of
enjoying peace of soul would then be to desire nothing.

Monsieur Vincent: 'Mademoiselle, be pleased to tell us
what you think.'

'One of the thoughts which came into my mind,
Father, in addition to what the Sisters have already said,
was this: God desires to be glorified in us in every way
possible; which indeed he is, when he makes use of us as,
by many titles, belonging to him; and so he can enable
us to do whatever he pleases; but he desires that we should
co-operate with his will, and it is very proper that we
should sacrifice to him the free will that he has given us,
and that by this means we should put ourselves into this
state of holy indifference in all those occupations in
which it shall please his goodness to put us by means of
the orders of our Superiors.

'Another thought is that, since we are given to God
to form a body within his Church, it is right that each
member should perform her function; which she could
not do if she were not submissive to the orders of the
Superior, who is the head of the body.

'The drawbacks which might arise from this would be:

First, the harm that such a Sister would do to herself, by putting herself in a condition of not being able to accomplish the will of God, nor of doing anything which could please him. Another: that without this holy indifference there would be disorder in the Company, the service of the poor would suffer, and a bad example would be given to the other Sisters, which some of them indeed might follow.

'One of the most powerful means that we have to help us to acquire this indifference is the example of our Lord, who during his life on earth testified in so many places that he was here on earth only to practise this virtue by doing the will of God his Father, and who persevered in his obedience for thirty years.'

Vincent de Paul: 'May God bless you, Mademoiselle! How beautifully that is expressed!'

Another Sister suggested that since the Daughters of Charity were given to God, it no longer belonged to them to desire to be this or that, to be in this place or somewhere else. If they should perform any act implying a right of (self-) ownership, they would be withdrawing themselves from God by a sort of robbery. We must therefore allow ourselves to be bent like the willow which the wickerwork woman twists in every direction, to make of it what she will.

Vincent de Paul: 'Can you give yet another reason, Sister?'

'Father, I have further observed that we should allow ourselves to be bent like the willow, so that the basket maker may make what he will.'

'That is what our Sister has just said. The Sisters of Charity should be as supple as the willow in the hands of him who uses her. The willow allows itself to be bent according to the will of the basket-maker, up and down; it does not resist. In the same way, a Daughter of Charity who is not in this state of indifference, who does not allow her superiors to post her where they will, in this

place or the other, whether as servant or companion, is
not as docile as the willow, nor so agreeable to God,
because she has not the suppleness which even a non-
rational object has. Oh, Sisters, what a confusion it is to
see a girl full of reasons!'

Other Sisters, and sometimes several at one time, would
speak in testimony of the virtue of indifference. In conclusion,
it would be the turn of Monsieur Vincent to deliver his
'little thoughts' and to conclude. In his view, the Daughters
of Charity ought to be indifferent, always available, like the
angels who stand before God ready at all times to do his
bidding. The Daughters are the angels of the charity of
God. Those who were perhaps not in this fitting state of
indifference, who might be harbouring in their hearts mere
personal desires, would shortly see those desires transformed
into passions which would agitate them as demons are
agitated. Monsieur Vincent concludes with a fervent prayer,
calling on God to preserve the Daughters from the wiles of
the devil; and to give them and sustain in them the angelic
spirit of indifference.

When any of the Sisters were about to depart to another
house, Monsieur Vincent and Mademoiselle would profit by
the occasion to discourse on the appropriate virtues, according to the nature of the place to which they were going and
the difficulties they would meet on the road, or when they
arrived.

Upon the death of a servant of the poor—a common event
in those early days, when the work was hard, and the zeal
of youth unrestrained—Monsieur Vincent and Louise took
occasion to base the conferences on the virtues of the Sister
who had gone to receive her reward. There was a most
beautiful and moving conference of this kind on Sister
Barbara Angiboust, one of the most outstanding figures of
the first generation of the movement, ardent, individualistic
to the extent of breaking at times a framework of rules still
ill-defined, and literally burned out by her love for God and

his poor. In 1658 she died, a martyr to her devotion at the hospital in Châteaudun. Those who had known her, those who had had the happiness of living with her came forward to testify how energetic she had been, how cheerful and good, how blunt in her goodwill. She it was who had refused her services to the duchesse d'Aiguillon and dared tell her why to her face: she was not one of the poor, and the poor should come before the rich of this world. Barbara had a special tenderness for small children. In the early days of great misery at the Enfants-Trouvés when there were not even enough cradles, Barbara would sleep with the babies in her arms. She knew how to talk to any child from the very moment that its mind awoke and her manner of catechising was quite exquisite. She succeeded in mastering her ardent nature, bringing it into subjection to the letter of the Rule; and she could handle with patience the most difficult of her poor—the prisoners in the galleys—despite their violence and their coarse habits. A citation from the record of what was said on this occasion will be of interest:

'I was with her among the prisoners in the galleys. She displayed great patience in bearing the hardships which are met with there, and which are due to the bad dispositions of those people. For although they were sometimes enraged with her, to the point of throwing the soup at her, and trampling the meat on the ground, saying to her whatever their impatience suggested, she suffered those things without a word, and patiently picked the things up with as sweet a grace as though they had said and done nothing to her.'

'Oh, that was the way to behave: to treat them just as before.'

'And not only that, Father. More than once, she prevented the guards from beating them.'

'Well, my Sisters, if there be any here who have worked among the prisoners in the galleys, and have felt like standing up to them and being rough with the

poor fellows, rendering evil for evil, and curse for curse,
grieve, and be sorry, seeing that one of your Sisters, who
wore the same habit as yourselves, when they threw at
her the meat she brought them, said not a word, and
when they were to be beaten, could not endure it. What
a reason for grief this should be to those who have acted
differently, and who anwer railing with railing when they
are dealing with those poor convicts and their guards!

'My Sisters, any of you who are here may at any time
be sent to serve those poor men. Learn then from our
Sister the lesson of how you ought to behave, not only
among the prisoners in the galleys, but everywhere else.'

All these features make up a portrait of Barbara Angiboust,
the beauty of which Monsieur Vincent greatly admired.
One of the Sisters remarked that mankind should wonder at
the Artist who had painted such a masterpiece; for it was a
work of God and of his grace. Monsieur Vincent then
turned to Louise, and asked whether she wished to add any
touches to the picture.

'Mademoiselle, will you please tell us what you yourself
observed?'

'I acknowledge, Father, that all that our Sisters have
said is true. She loved all points which touched the Rule,
and was greatly attracted to the teaching of the young.
From the moment she became acquainted with the Rule,
she never desired to omit anything from what was commanded, or to innovate in any way whatever.

'Wherever she went, even at the Enfants-Trouvés,
which place she visited more than once, I never saw her
shrink from anything. When the news of her death was
made known, reports of her virtues came in from all the
places which she had served.

'When she wrote to me, she would sign herself "The
Proud One", out of the desire that she had for humility,
at which she laboured without ceasing.

'She was a tower of strength to the Sisters wherever

she might be. One of these, who had been with her at
Châteaudun, having on some occasion been a sore trial
to her, was afterwards sorry for it, and begged her
pardon. When this Sister saw Barbara lying ill of the
sickness of which she was to die, she spoke of that matter
(and Barbara replied): "Sister, was it not necessary that
it should be so?", as though to say, "It is by bearing
with them that we win over those who are carried away
by some impulse contrary to duty."

'Our Sisters who lived with her in her last days have
informed me that they observed in her so many virtues
that eight quires of paper would not suffice to describe
them.

'I never saw her deflected from her resolutions. She
loved the Company very dearly, and sorrowed grievously
whenever she heard of any matter that was not for the
good of the community.

'Here is the letter by which I was notified of her death:
"You will have learned of the death of our dear Sister
Barbara by the letter we sent you. We confirm to you by
the present letter that she died in God, etc." Father,
there came a woman from Châteaudun who assisted her
at her death, who told us all that that letter tells us, and
among other things that, had she not witnessed her
passing, she would not have recognised her after her
death, so beautiful was she: "which is what is written in
the letter"—but such was her beauty that some people
said she was made up.

'Well, my Sisters, what a beautiful picture! We may
be happy that we have lived with a soul given to the
practice of such virtues!'

One of the most attractive features of these conferences is
the absence of all formality. Everything is seen clearly, as in
the fresh light of dawn, and each Sister says what she has to
say in her own way, in her 'proud country tongue' so that,
though the word is never used, a great demonstration of

truth may be gathered from the collection. The Daughter of Charity, formed by these instructions, is essentially *true*.

Nourished on the inspired teaching of these discourses— a teaching in part her own—and drawing upon her own stores, which were rich, Louise de Marillac continued the formation of her Daughters in Conferences of her own composition. Following the example of her 'much-honoured Father' she avoided all formalism and spoke in familiar terms according to the circumstances. For this reason no formal minutes of her conferences have come down to us. But the book of prayers in use in the Congregation throws a flood of light upon a theme which must have provided the framework and the texture of her teaching: this was the liturgy and the liturgical year. What Louise has to say on the feast of the day is not only very solid theology, but her love of the liturgy shines through every word.

I might have made a study of this subject at this point, to complete our analysis of her method of instructing her Daughters; but we shall arrive at a better understanding of her original and intimate qualities if we defer such consideration until we come to deal with the rich vein of her private spirituality. When her life was drawing to its close she was no longer directly concerned with the formation of her Daughters; but she lived with them, prayed with them and for them. This is the exquisite feature of the teaching activity of the saints: to teach, they have but to be themselves.

A TEACHER STILL

LOUISE DE MARILLAC had a gift for imparting instruction, a passionate love of teaching, for she valued knowledge and prized wisdom for which man was made. God created us that we might *know* him; he made us so that he might himself be known by intelligent beings. Ignorance is therefore a condition of violence which holds man back from his destiny.

At his first contact with the people of those country districts devastated by the wars, Vincent de Paul was appalled by material misery: they were dying of hunger! Thirty years later Louise de Marillac, travelling through the same countryside and observing particularly the women and girls, was appalled by their rude illiteracy.

There had for some years now been observed in France a new stirring of intellectual life. In the course of the seventeenth century it was to reinvigorate the old congregations, call new ones into being and produce a succession of gifted and practical teachers.* So wide and deep was the influence of this movement that those historians who are now approaching the subject are astonished at the sound education of the women of the French upper and middle classes in this period. But the teaching of the lower classes was still seriously neglected. It was taken for granted that country children and especially country girls had no need of reading.

Louise de Marillac was horrified by a neglect which could have such terrible consequences. Her argument should be noted with care. She feared that little girls allowed to grow up in ignorance would be unable to benefit from the gifts of God. Of course, she did not hold that the efficacy of God's grace could ever depend on human knowledge, but she had

(*) A brief but enlightening discussion of this subject may be found in: Barnard (H.C.), 'Girls at School under the *Ancien Régime*', 1954.

observed that elementary knowledge opens a way for the teaching of the Church and sets this teaching in a human, social context which makes it more accessible and more appealing. One can love God without knowing how to read; but a knowledge of reading supplies additional motives for loving God and means of profiting more fully from his grace. So, as soon as she began her systematic visiting of the Charities Louise took care to gather information relating to the children and about any person in the locality who could teach them to read.

Such a step was of course a mere stop-gap. Teaching must be organised—and Louise had a gift for organisation. Now we come to a document of considerable significance; it marks the foundation on May 29th, 1641, of free elementary schools in the diocese of Paris. Here Louise de Marillac makes a formal approach to the Precentor of the Cathedral of Notre-Dame, who was responsible for public education in the city.

'To M. des Roches, precentor of Notre-Dame de Paris, Louise de Marillac, widow of M. Le Gras, secretary to the queen-mother of the King, most humbly petitions:

'And says that great numbers of the poor in the Faubourg de Saint-Denis have made her desire to undertake to teach them; for the reason that if the poor little girls remain in ignorance, it is much to be feared that this will lead them into malice, which will render them incapable of co-operating with grace for their own salvation. The which considering, may it please you, Monsieur, to give the said petitioner the warranty required for such activity, in the hope that God will be glorified if the poor, giving nothing, may freely send their children to the schools; and that no wealthy person may be able to prevent such a benefit, merely because they do not desire that the mistresses who teach their own children should receive the children of the poor.

'These souls, purchased by the Blood of the Son of

God, will be bound to pray for you, Monsieur, through
time and through eternity.'

The Reverend Precentor replied as follows:

'Michel Le Masle, counsellor to the King in all his
Councils of State and private councils, prior, and
Seigneur des Roches de Saint-Paul, precentor and
Canon of the glorious metropolitan church of Paris, to
our well beloved Demoiselle Le Gras, dwelling in the
parish of Saint-Laurent at Paris, health in Our Lord.

'Whereas it belongs to us, by reason of our dignity as
Precentor of the said church of Paris, to have the scrutiny
and government of the elementary schools of the city,
suburbs and environs of Paris; and whereas you have
been found worthy to keep schools; our investigation
having been made, with the testimonial of your parish
priest, and of other persons worthy of credit; and having
knowledge of your manner of life and your Catholic
faith;

'We therefore grant you licence for this purpose, and
give our faculty to you, to keep and maintain schools in
the street known as Saint-Lazare in the Faubourg Saint-
Denis, for the office of teaching poor girls only, and none
others, and to bring them up in good manners, in the
rules of grammar, and other pious and useful exercise,
having first taken your oath to conduct the said schools
diligently and faithfully according to our statutes and
ordinances.

'This present faculty is valid only until our next Synod.

'Given at Paris under our seal, and that of Maître
Jean Le Vasseur, notary apostolic and our writer and
secretary in ordinary, in the year of our Lord sixteen
hundred and forty-one, on the twenty-ninth day of May.

By command of my said Lord Precentor,

LE VASSEUR.'

And so popular education for the poor girls of Paris was
introduced. Primary education for poor boys was to come a

little later with St John Baptist de La Salle. Both systems developed together throughout the seventeenth century, at the same pace as the schools for the privileged classes and both flourish vigorously to this day.

For Louise de Marillac these schools for the poor were one of the forms of charity, and her correspondence with Sister Turgis at Angers is full of exhortations to be ever mindful of her duty of supervising the behaviour of the children and the good order of the schools. She consulted Monsieur Vincent on the subject and he at once recognised the importance of the work. He expressed the desire that some uniformity of method might be introduced; that the Sisters of the mother house might be trained in this method; and that they should take the advice of the Ursulines, who had wide experience in such work. It is true that the care of the sick and the service of the poor have always been the principal activities of the Daughters of Charity, and that they are always willing to relinquish work in the schools wherever it can be left with confidence in other Christian hands; yet to serve the poor means filling his real needs, be they of mind or body.

Louise herself may have been the first of these school-mistresses. She tells us nothing of the methods she used for teaching little children their letters; but we are left in no doubt of her preoccupation with methods of teaching them Christian doctrine. She appears to have been less than satisfied with the forms of catechism then in use, for she compiled a catechism of her own, the manuscript of which is preserved in the archives of the mother house. This is not so much a manual as a personal directory, a quest for words and forms which will gradually introduce the truths of religion to the most infantile and immature minds. As we thumb through this manual we note her uncertainties and her false starts and also her striking insights. Expressions familiarly used of the most everyday application are always linked with some very secure dogmatic statement. She taught the mysteries with a smile:

'What is the mystery of the Blessed Trinity?

'It is the mystery of One God in three Persons, Father,
    Son and Holy Spirit.'

'And of these three, which is the oldest and most wise?'

'All three are equal, for they are but one and the same
    God.'

The little foundlings of Bicêtre, the beggar children of
Saint-Denis, heard her speak of God in their own language.
Forms of speech change with time, but the problems of
speech are constant and catechists of today might well draw
inspiration from the mind of Louise de Marillac. All round
us today there are children as far from God as the children
of 1641.

Louise could chatter with the children; she could speak
their own language with ladies of rank. We would like to
dwell upon her relations with the great, but it is not easy to
do so, for she never made any show of these friendships—or
rather, she deliberately concealed them; and since it is here
a question of the secrets of the heart, or of heart-to-heart, the
ladies who had the benefit of her friendship have left little
on record. But allusions made by Louise in her correspondence with Vincent de Paul are so numerous as to give
the impression of one of her major works.

Mademoiselle's relations with women of rank outside her
own family circle sprang out of that spiritual movement, the
central figure in which had been her father's brother, Michel
de Marillac. At that time her contacts with society women
had been more frequent, as Monsieur Vincent had appointed
her to visit the Charities and in these the Ladies had taken
the lead. Later she had found herself virtually a member of
the Company of Ladies of the Hôtel-Dieu, where she was in
close and regular contact with the best-known members of
the aristocracy and the upper middle class. It was not very
long before she held a special position among them, along
with such personages as Mme la Présidente Goussault and
Mme Viole. Always available and always ready to undertake

practical tasks, Louise was more and more called upon,
especially after she had organised her Daughters into a permanent Congregation specialising in the care of the sick.

But for those women who were seeking progress in their
spiritual life she was something more: a pattern, an inspiration and a guide. In her childhood she had acquired a store
of profane learning, which quickened her language and
adorned her thought in a style reminiscent of Mme de Sablé,
Mme de La Fayette, or even Mme de Sévigné. Her spiritual
reading was even wider: Luis of Granada, Bérulle, François
de Sales, the Gospels—all had enriched her mind. She had
been accorded the faculty rarely granted to women in her
day of reading the Bible in an unabridged French version.
These things are evidence of a mature spirituality, and we
need not therefore wonder that eminent women,* knowing
the extent and value of her spirituality, sought to benefit from
it by spending days of recollection under her guidance. They
recognised in her not a nun withdrawn from the world but a
woman who had been married and borne a child, who had
suffered and overcome many troubles, both outwardly and
inwardly. She was experienced in the ways of the world and
the life of the spirit and was therefore well fitted to direct a
house of retreat.

The mother house of the Daughters of Charity now began
to be used in part as a house of retreat. Monsieur Vincent
was ordinarily somewhat strict upon such a point, but he
gave her every encouragement to persevere in this new
activity which is of a kind not, as a rule, suited to a woman.
But Louise, when she conducted her retreats for ladies,
followed Monsieur Vincent's guidance very exactly and
would even request him to draw up a detailed timetable.
Yet this would turn out to be no more than a timetable:
Monsieur Vincent meant Louise to conduct the retreats by
herself.

(*) The correspondence mentions Mme de Mirepoix, Mme de Traversay,
Mlle Polaillon, and the Duchesses de Liancourt and de Ventadour.

So in conversation and in prayer she dispensed the riches of her heart; the ladies who came to enjoy those riches maintained contact with her, so as to be sure always of her direct and dependable guidance.

It was not just ordinary friendship which bound Louise to such women as the Duchesse de Ventadour and the Duchesse de Liancourt; when they heard of her mortal illness they flatly refused to leave her and installed themselves to assist her last moments and be with her when she died.

THE DRAMA OF THE 'ENFANTS TROUVÉS'

WE MAY well speak of drama in connection with the *Enfants Trouvés*—a social drama, since the civil authorities had signally failed to heal a bleeding wound in the side of the nation; a human drama, because helpless children were abandoned to wretchedness and death; a personal drama, because the state of those waifs and strays ravaged the heart of Louise with immense sorrow. It is to the glory of Monsieur Vincent and Mademoiselle that they refused to accept the situation and fought with deeds against the stubbornness of official opinion until they had created an atmosphere in which, little by little, remedies were found.

The depths of human selfishness will never be plumbed. Civil commotion, social hypocrisy and public misery all found their most defenceless victims in the children of France. Thousands, deserted in the fratricidal wars, were abandoned to public charity. Vice paid homage to virtue and exploited it, and when an infant was left at a church door the deserter salved his conscience by leaning on the generosity of charitable people. Everything, even the deeds of the good, weighed most heavily on the children.

The origins of the *Enfants Trouvés* are still obscure. It is known that in Paris, about the year 1600, nearly four hundred infants were abandoned each year. They were taken in either by charitable individuals or by the sergeants of the justices. In 1630 a house, vulgarly known as '*La Couche*' (i.e. 'the napkin'), was acquired for their accommodation. Responsibility for their care was divided between a committee representing the great religious orders and the Chapter of Notre-Dame, and it is to be feared that each of these parties relied upon the other to maintain the place. Conditions were terrible. There was not enough room, there were not enough nurses, there was not enough of anything. Babies died in great numbers and every child in the house was ill and suffering. There soon grew up a most odious traffic: the children were hired out or sold to ruffians who broke their legs to cripple them and thus excite pity and extort alms. It was no easy matter to launch a crusade against this dreadful scourge, so dishonouring to humanity and to Christian conscience. Vast resources would be required; social prejudice against doing anything for bastard children would have to be overcome; and it was to be feared that, in adopting these children, other desertions would be encouraged.

Vincent de Paul and Louise de Marillac dared the venture. From the outset they put into it their entire and only wealth and strength—human compassion and practical ability. After a careful preliminary enquiry, Louise drew up a memorandum which Monsieur Vincent amplified, revised and approved. Both decided to enlist for this work the services of the Society of Ladies of the Hôtel-Dieu—at that time, like the congregation of the Daughters of Charity, in the first enthusiasm of youth. At the annual meeting in 1640, there were gathered together the most eminent women of the Parisian aristocracy and bourgeoisie, the central figures being the duchesse d'Aiguillon and the princesse de Condé. If this fearful emergency were to be dealt with, all Paris must be mobilised.

The project presented to the meeting by Vincent de Paul was well received. It was resolved that half-measures should be dropped, and that they should aim high: that is to say, take over the entire organisation of the *Enfants Trouvés*; the Ladies should deal with general administration and the Daughters of Charity provide the practical organisation and the hands for the work. Procedure was to be the same as in any great collective effort: the administration would discuss and vote, and leave the carrying out of decisions to the secretary-general; and the secretary-general was, in effect,

Louise de Marillac. Upon her and upon Monsieur Vincent fell the burden and heat of the day.

When the plan was made public, enthusiasm was enormous, and Louise was much encouraged. King Louis XIII bestowed on the work a pension of 4,000 *livres*, a sum which Anne of Austria followed and doubled. Yet even with an assured income of this amount, it was soon obvious that a budget of 40,000 *livres* annually was the absolute minimum needed to keep the work going. They had been sadly wide of the mark in their calculations. The deficit would have to be made up from alms and from subscriptions from the Ladies. It was necessary to recall backsliders, to remind each of her promises and her responsibilities, to call meetings, to be very grateful for services and gifts in kind, to soothe susceptibilities and smooth ruffled vanity.

What was to be done with the children? Louise's improvisations were marked by a touch of genius. Reception centres were set up at points far apart: one of these, of course, would be a house of the Daughters of Charity, first at La Chapelle, later in the Rue Saint-Denis. These centres proved inadequate and placing in private families was tried. The Charities and the parish clergy drew up lists of families and individuals to whom the care of a child might safely be entrusted. The child then set off to one of these foster-parents, along with his bill of health. Some of these have survived, a few being in Monsieur Vincent's own hand, with the address of the foster-parents written in the margin. The bill of health had to be kept up to date by the foster-parents, and scrutinised at regular intervals by the parish priest or the nearest Charity. The Ladies, with a Daughter to assist, paid frequent visits to each home, took notes and sent in reports. Children thus cared for, growing up in wholesome and humane conditions and watched over might be said to be saved. They were not only protected but loved, and it was love that fitted them for a normal life in society. It happened frequently that enduring bonds were formed between the boys and girls and the families that had adopted them: the unclassed were re-classed, and delivered from the burden of their birth.*

La Couche, with all the private homes which rallied to the work, soon proved to be hopelessly inadequate. Placing in families soon reached a limit. The Ladies were ambitious to provide something better, larger and more capable of adaptation to ever growing needs. The Château de Bicêtre, vast and solemn, was vacant and available. If only it were theirs. Could they approach the Queen, to whom all things were possible? Monsieur Vincent would be sure of success. Negotiations were opened in 1643.

This was a matter in which Louise de Marillac was at variance with the Ladies of Charity. In a careful and courageous letter to Monsieur Vincent, she set out her objections. Bicêtre, she said, was much too far from Paris; the Château, like every house that has had negligent owners, was dilapidated: it would cost a great deal to put it in order and it would never be really suitable for the work. The Daughters appointed to care for the children there would be for ever on the roads between Bicêtre and Paris, which was no part of their vocation. Having thus expressed her opinion, Louise said no more. When the Château was handed over to the Ladies, she exerted herself to put the place in order and her organising gifts had plenty of scope.

To bring the children from the Hôtel-Dieu to Bicêtre a horse and light cart would be required, with a man to drive. The roads were bad and the little ones were exhausted by travelling in the carts and wagons then in common use. Often a Daughter, touched with pity, would pick a child up from the lurching dog-cart and trudge along behind with him on her shoulders.

(*) To a generation familiar with the United Nations Organisation, the particulars of the organisation of *Les Enfants Trouvés* appear almost common-place. It cannot be too frequently stressed that here, as in so many other ways, Louise was an innovator of genius. None of this structure existed before she created it, and every modern charitable enterprise owes something of its methods and perhaps all of its spirit to her.

As soon as possible, the house at Bicêtre must be made self-supporting. There was land; it would have to be cultivated. There were vineyards and the wine could be sold, since neither the Daughters nor the children drank it. Wheat they could buy, and a bakery would have to be built, with a baker to bake them nourishing bread. Some of the rooms in the house were very large; they could be adapted and fitted as class-rooms. Thus were the schools brought into being, precise and a little limited as to the education they bestowed, modelled on that of the Ursulines; precise, too, in discipline, which was maternal and firm, tending to severity. Once they were five the children were taught to read. At eleven, the boys were apprenticed. The girls remained in the home, learning domestic work, until they could be placed in service. We should bear these details in mind: they have their historical significance and they formed a character of a certain type.

Life in a home depends on the wisdom of the rules and especially on the warmth of those who apply them. Louise knew that for work with the foundlings she would need Daughters of a special cast. With Monsieur Vincent's agreement she set about forming them. How touching and noble were the words addressed by Vincent to a group of girls destined for the work, in a conference on December 7th, 1643. We would be tempted to see Louise's touch in them if we did not know that Vincent, too, was possessed of great tenderness. He told them that to be appointed to the service of these waifs was like receiving a patent of nobility. Since their parents had abandoned them they were children of God, who had lovingly welcomed them and entrusted them to the Daughters who, like Mary, were to be both virgins and mothers. Happy were they that they had been chosen for this work.

'If God had not called you to his service, if he had left you in the midst of the turmoils of the world, you yourselves would have become mothers, and your children

E

would have given you far more trouble and anxiety than
these will do. And to what advantage? Like most other
mothers, you would have loved them with a natural
love. What then would have been your recompense? The
recompense of nature—your own satisfaction. If these,
now, were the children of noble families, you would be
put to a lot of trouble—more, perhaps, than these will
give you: and your recompense? Salaries—on the small
side. And your positions would be those of servants. But
after you have served these infants which the world
abandons, what will be your recompense?—God, in
eternity.

The children themselves would become their recompense.
Abandoned they would have died or grown up to be rogues.
Brought up by them, they would become the founders of
Christian families. Their duty to these children was sacred;
they must truly be mothers to them.

'Mothers have no greater consolation than to watch
the little activities of their children. They love and
admire everything their children do. They would expose
themselves to any evil, to save their children a little pain.

'Mothers in tenderness, you will be their angels, to
preserve them from evil and train them in all things good.

'You ought above all things to fear giving any scandal
to these poor children, to do or say any wrong thing
before them. If Mademoiselle Le Gras could have angels
in her service, she would have to give them up to serve
these innocents. There is a story going round that we are
only sending [to Bicêtre] those Daughters who are no use
at other work. Quite the contrary: at Bicêtre we shall
want the most able and most virtuous Daughters that we
have; for the children will be what their "aunts" are. If
the "aunt" is good, the children will be good; if the
"aunt" is bad, the children will be so, because they so
easily follow example. If you lose your tempers, they
will become bad-tempered. If you slip into petty faults

before them, they will do the same; if you grumble, they will grumble.'

The conference ended with advice on religious training, precise and tender in its penetration.

Louise de Marillac was often at Bicêtre. She worked with all her heart to make the place a success, though she was sorely tried by the inconveniences which she had foreseen. In a letter to Monsieur Vincent, she made her complaint with a slight edge of ill-humour:

'Now, as to the letter from Mme de Pollalion giving a testimonial for this man who offers his services for Bicêtre. He says that he is very good at making bread, garden work, ploughing and carting. All this work has to be done out there, and it works out very dear when it has to be done by the day.

'Fifty-two children have died in Bicêtre since we went there, and there are fifteen or sixteen others who are not doing very well. I hope that when all is conveniently arranged, according to the wishes of these good Ladies, the children will not leave us so quickly. Perhaps they will tell you that I have spoken of the necessity of having the Blessed Sacrament out here, not only for cases of need, but so that our Lord may take possession of the house in the sight of all who are in any way concerned with the work of the place: a point on which I take the liberty to tell you that it came into my mind, that not only should the Ladies be advised of the day, but it should also be given out clearly in the parish notices, so that the people may come and support our intentions. When people see this magnificent pile, and hear that it is given over to little children, and that all who are responsible for it are of high position, most of them think there must be plenty of money for all our needs—whereas the fact is, that we have to borrow to buy in the provisions for the week, in addition to all our other needs, as you well know.

'May it please you, of your charity, to remember to
ask for some more girls to help us, as our need of them is
very urgent, the work of the house increasing every day.'
All the correspondence of Louise between 1646 and 1651
is filled with stifled complaint and heartrending appeals.
She had now given herself entirely over to the work of the
Enfants Trouvés, with something amounting to passion. The
needs of the Château increased with every hour, but income
lessened. Monsieur Vincent's zeal certainly did not wane,
but he was overwhelmed by the widespread misery throughout the provinces. Ladies of Charity were tired of giving—
and the limits of begging had been reached. Everyone began
to make excuses. Political disorder was returning to the
country, and the Fronde was inflaming tempers and closing
hearts everywhere. And at this most anxious time, Monsieur
Vincent was absent in the country.

Louise de Marillac missed her director sorely. But more
important, her children were becoming more and more
hungry. At last, on December 15th, 1648, Louise appealed to
Mademoiselle de Lamoignon, a woman of unbounded
generosity, a remarkable Christian totally unable to hate
anyone, not even the devil himself, a woman who knew only
love and generosity. Louise begged for counsel and support:

'I beg pardon that I have not written to Mme Séguier
as you instructed me to do. I believe I have talked only
too much about the extreme needs of these poor children
and their nurses, even to the point of being importunate
with several persons, saddening too much, perhaps,
hearts which have been sympathetic and charitable.
There remains nothing for me to tell you, except that I
seem to see the Ladies of the Company, who are much
more mothers to these little ones than their own mothers
ever were, plunged into the righteous grief of the mothers
of the Innocents at the massacre, because they are
quite without power to do anything to help. We must, all

the same, expect from the bounty of Providence some
notable form of help, such as was lately provided for
some little new arrivals who had just been found (may
God be eternally praised for it).

'I believe, Mademoiselle, that you are shortly going
to call a large meeting. Would it not be a good thing to
reconsider the notices already sent out for taking collections every Saturday in Notre Dame, and on first Sundays
and major feasts in the churches of every suburb and
town? Perhaps the Ladies as a body would undertake
this duty each in their own district. Those who undertook to be on duty could take neighbours or friends to
help them, and so it would not be a very great burden.
It will be said that such an effort would bring in but
little; in particular places that might be so, but the total
effort would bring in something. The gentlemen down
at the office must be getting some advantage from it, for
they are always getting up these same collections.

'I believe also, Mademoiselle, that you will speak of
the great need there is of help to keep the little breakfasts
going at the Hôtel-Dieu. They are more necessary than
ever. Those poor people sometimes tell me that the
breakfast is the only meal they get; and surely it is their
only pleasure.

'Do you not recall, Mademoiselle, that when this work
began, the Ladies on the administration reported on all
the good, spiritual and material, that came of making
visits in connection with the breakfasts? By this means,
the Ladies were able to see the good results of their visits
and alms. This might perhaps be done again. But I am
in dread that this work may fail, and this fear drives me
to take the liberty of making these suggestions. You will,
if you please, pardon her who is, with all her heart, in the
love of our Lord. . . .'

But Mlle de Lamoignon was no longer able to give any
help: her house had been a storehouse for the poor but now

it was empty. Christmas was now very near, and the Hôtel-Dieu had no flour; the children would not eat even bread on the holy days. Now the most open-handed of the Ladies had left Paris and there was no one left to whom appeal could be made: he who is ashamed that he can give no more will hide himself away. And then Louise thought of the highest financial authority in the land—Pierre Séguier, the Chancellor of France—difficult of access, but a man of great soul. She addressed to him an appeal which is full of nobility.

'The respect which I owe to Your Highness bids me remember those occasions when I collected the charity Your Highness had promised at Saint-Germain to the poor foundlings.

'But seeing, Monseigneur, that all has failed, I take the liberty of these lines, since I am not able to do myself the honour of seeking you out myself, to represent to you that there are a hundred of these poor little children; that among all their present necessities, the one that weighs upon me most is that they have no bread against the festival; that this matter burdens my heart so heavily that I should fear, Monseigneur, being too much guilty, if any consideration should prevent me from having recourse to Your Highness, who on so many other occasions has seemed to be truly the succour of the poor.

'Permit me, then, this great boldness, and to sign myself with every kind of submission and respect, in the Love of God for whom you act. . . .'

One would like to believe that Séguier gave bread for the foundlings that Christmastide of 1684, and that he had abundance for himself.

Peace, transitory and insecure, returned to France. Monsieur Vincent and the Ladies came back to Paris. Louise had a breathing-space, but the *Enfants Trouvés* had fallen very low and means were lacking to carry the work forward. The fortunes of the Ladies, which consisted for the most part of land, were ruined and would be so for years to come, for the war had laid waste the country around Paris. Louise, absorbed in her poor and her foundlings, was perhaps not able to appreciate the extent of the catastrophe and was at times unjust in her complaints. Monsieur Vincent saw the whole picture more clearly and declared that he was most reluctant to appeal again, for fear of becoming a nuisance.

In October 1649, the distress at the *Enfants Trouvés* reached its peak. Louise, at the end of her strength, began to say she would have to let everything go. She wrote to Monsieur Vincent:

'I am very importunate, but we have reached the point where we must have help without delay, or give up everything. Yesterday, we had to deal out all the housekeeping money, fifteen to twenty *livres*, and then borrow more, to buy wheat for the children at Bicêtre and we cannot depend upon receiving anything whatever in a month's time. There are now a dozen or thirteen babies here and not a scrap of linen to change them. It is essential, if you please, that at the meeting of the Ladies something should be done, and preferably that they put into effect that resolution about collecting in the parishes every Sunday, setting up little money-boxes in the churches in prominent places, and seeing that the clergy and preachers draw attention to them, and taking up collections outside the church as well, as was proposed. I believe that if somebody went to see the Princess about these extreme needs, she would give something. May it please your charity to let us know if they are sending us tickets for the meeting, and if you think it would be well to invite to it Mme de Schomberg and Mme de Verthamont. For the rest of what I had to tell you, it would take too long; it will be more quickly done in a few words tomorrow, if I have the honour of seeing you. I stand in very great need of the particular assistance of God at this time, for wherever I turn, and whatever I put my hand to,

I see nothing but misery and affliction. God be praised! It is enough that I tell you the great need I have of your charity, as it has pleased Providence that I should be. . . .'

If we are to be in full sympathy with the tone of this letter, we must bear in mind that civil affairs were at this time in a state of total collapse.

In the midst of the commotion and confusion left behind by the retreating armies of 1648, others were preoccupied with their own immediate worries, and Louise de Marillac stood practically alone to deal with the administrative details of every day. It was she who must discover that the bread had run out, she who found that there was no linen to change the babies; she who took in the new mouths, brought every day and left with her.

All this excuses her growing impatience and in the end her resignation of her post.

'I am extremely vexed to have to be so importunate with you, but the sheer impossibility of taking in any more of these children is too heavy a burden. We have at present seven babies who will no longer take the feeding-bottle, and I have no double who could nurse them; we have no more reserves of baby linen at all, no sheets, and not a hope of borrowing any more. Do us the charity, my much honoured Father, to advise us whether we can in conscience expose them to death, for the Ladies are no longer exerting themselves to get us help, and I declare I believe they think we are doing everything here at their expense, which is very far from the truth. I know of only one way to relieve all those who are suffering under this work: in the name of our Company, we must present a petition to the First-President, that we be exempted from taking in any more of these children. But the consent of the Ladies will have to be gained for this request, so that there be no scandal; without such exemption, it seems to me we shall all be in constant mortal sin.

'Four babies were brought here yesterday, and in addition to seven at the breast, there are three weaned babies newly found, and we shall have to put them out to nurse again, if we can; if I could carry this burden without making you share it, I would do so very willingly but our helpless condition will not allow it. The good Ladies are not doing what they could; not one of them has sent anything, nor do we receive anything from those of the Company. I begin to fear that all this wretchedness comes on my account, who am such as I am, my much honoured Father, your very obliged and very obedient Daughter.'

Her cry was heard. Monsieur Vincent called the full meeting of the Ladies. He described to them the state of distress at the *Enfants Trouvés* and, like Louise, he spoke of throwing up the work. He gave an account of the prevailing misery; but he also indicated to the assembled Ladies one last means by which everything could be saved: their curios and trinkets, those expensive trifles for which they really cared nothing, and their jewels, would bring in some money. The Queen had given him a necklace and a royal example they could surely follow. He ended this conference with the celebrated words now known to all the world. We reproduce them here, in pages consecrated to Louise de Marillac, because these words sprang from the heart of the mother of the Foundlings, just as much as from the heart of their father, Vincent de Paul; and because of the honour they confer upon all that is Christian and humane in France.

'Now, Ladies, compassion and charity have led you to adopt these little creatures as your own children. You have been their mothers according to grace, because their mothers in nature have deserted them. Now, see if you also will abandon them? Cease for a little while to be their mothers, and become for a moment their judges; life and death for them is in your hands; I am about to take your votes and sentences; it is time to pronounce

judgment on them, and to find out whether you no
longer wish to have mercy on them. If you continue your
charitable care they will live; on the other hand, if you
abandon them, without fail they will die and perish:
of that, experience leaves you no room for doubt.'

There was no resisting such an appeal. Yet again the work
of the *Enfants Trouvés* was saved by the sacrifices of the Ladies.

Yet danger had not entirely disappeared. Disorder, and
a new famine, came back with the Second Fronde. This time,
the children and the Sisters were in bodily danger: fighting
took place in the neighbourhood of Bicêtre. Yet there was
more fear than danger. We still find in letters from Louise an
occasional appeal and a few complaints; after that, there is
little more talk of the *Enfants Trouvés*. The situation at
Bicêtre was stabilised and in course of time the work was
taken over again by the General Hospital.

For twenty years this vast undertaking had been Louise's
great preoccupation and anxiety. One would have said that
the work had worn out her heart, except that her heart was
enriched and strengthened by all she did. After 1650, the
tone of her voice changes, becomes more concentrated, less
passionate; but this is not age or spiritual fatigue. A new kind
of greatness was taking shape in her.

This chapter concerned with the enterprise of the *Enfants
Trouvés* should not be closed without a few words on two
similar works of mercy, in which Louise had been invited to
help: the Almshouse of the Name of Jesus, and the General
Hospital. We shall not even sketch their history, but just
draw attention to certain marks left upon these institutions
by the strong, discreet character of Mademoiselle.

About 1650, a wealthy citizen of Paris anonymously gave
to Monsieur Vincent the sum of 100,000 *livres*, for the establishment of a permanent work of mercy of his own choice.
Monsieur Vincent bought a piece of ground and a house,
which he converted for use as a hospital; he bestowed on
Saint-Lazare an income sufficient to maintain forty old -

people, twenty men and twenty women, chosen from workers whom old age or feebleness had rendered incapable of earning their own living. This was the Almshouse of the Name of Jesus. The founder's aim, apart from the obvious charitable one, was to set up a model almshouse and so to prove that it was possible to break with the inhumane routine of the older almshouses. At The Name of Jesus, the residents were clad in neat and suitable clothes and had each his own bed. There were a well-lighted chapel and refectory and the food was carefully prepared. The residents could not go out, but they could amuse themselves by following some occupation with which they were familiar and the profit from this would allow them to buy some little extra luxury, such as wine. All these simple details were innovations. Responsibility for the management of this almshouse devolved upon the Mission and it was natural that Monsieur Vincent should turn to Louise and her Daughters, to put the almshouse on a sound footing.

In a short note, Louise described to Monsieur Vincent the methodical way in which she set to work:

'The little family was assembled punctually, except for one man and one of the women, who had not yet arrived. But I believe, Monsieur, that it will be necessary for your charity to take the trouble to settle them down tomorrow morning with some devotional exercise, such as Adoration of the Holy Cross, and an exhortation of some sort on the Passion. It is bold of me to make such a suggestion. If it please your charity to give instructions, either this evening or early tomorrow morning, the clothes which have been got ready for them should be distributed.'

The chronicle of the house, the individual condition of each resident, the bookkeeping—all these details are recorded in a register, on the most modern lines.

Monsieur Vincent had a special affection for this alms-house, so well ordered and wisely governed. He paid the old people regular visits. A summary has been preserved of a discourse which he gave them on the sign of the Cross: 'This is how we make it'; and he made it, each gesture separately. 'Now I shall ask you to make it. If you do not know how, do not be ashamed. How many great lords there are about the Court, and perhaps even Presidents, who can do it no better than you. You will learn how to make it, and will learn, too, all the other things necessary to your salvation according to the desire of your benefactor, who has lodged you so comfortably in this house.'

The almshouse of The Name of Jesus was something of a wonder to the curious who came to see the place, but it caused a twinge of jealousy in some of the Ladies since they had had no share in founding or running the place, and the Daughters who worked there were removed from their jurisdiction.

The Ladies were cherishing a great project, which would far exceed in scope all those other works to which they had so generously contributed. The scheme was not of Vincentian inspiration, yet it was in a sense an extension of his activity, a consequence of that renewed impulse to charitable work which Vincent de Paul had set in motion and which had now been working fruitfully in the Christian conscience for thirty years.

The project sought to unify those more secular and sporadic efforts, made from time to time by the *Parlement*, by royalty, by the police, in the attempt to put down begging by housing the mendicants in institutions. This was an old problem, frequently attacked and as frequently defying all attempts at a solution. This time it was to be taken seriously. The Fronde had collapsed, the war was drawing to an end. Those works of charitable enterprise already launched now seemed to be in a fair way to succeed. They were all to be surpassed by this new venture. Money was being put into it: the duchesse d'Aiguillon promised 100,000 *livres*, and the Ladies, though not so grandly, imitated her example. Monsieur Vincent kept his thoughts to himself and was silent.

Louise de Marillac, having been approached by the Ladies, meditated, pen in hand. In substance, what she wrote was as follows: It may well be that the moment has come for our women to come out of the houses, to undertake a more public work for which they may shoulder the entire responsibility. Why should they not found the General Hospital? Assuredly, they would have to take counsel of competent and influential men, and they must be assured by the Superior of the Mission that he would take all responsibility on the spiritual side. It is evident that Monsieur Vincent saw this letter. If not entirely convinced, he was sufficiently won over to allow the matter to take its course. He exerted himself to obtain from the Queen the buildings of the Salpêtrière. With great enthusiasm, the work of restoration and adaptation was begun. The Ladies were jubilant.

Then, suddenly, the building stopped. The royal authorities expressed the opinion that an undertaking on this scale could not be allowed to remain entirely in the hands of a charitable society. A request was made that the Ladies should proceed no further. Their disappointment was bitter, but the Ladies had the heroism of devotion. The General Hospital became a municipal establishment in which their generosity played its part. Begging was suppressed by royal decree in 1657 and beggars were invited to let themselves be shut up in the General Hospital.

There were 40,000 mendicants in Paris alone, many among them blind or maimed. Upon publication of the decree by sudden miracle they found themselves cured and ready to look for work. Three-quarters of them left Paris for the country. For the moment the problem was solved. But it was to spring up again in each succeeding generation, as though the profession of begging were part of the nature of things.

The decree which established the General Hospital appointed the Mission to its spiritual direction and made the Daughters of Charity responsible for the care of the sick in the place. Monsieur Vincent declined to release for this work any of his own workers on the Mission, who were always in demand for his work elsewhere. Mademoiselle could only spare two or three of her Daughters to organise the care of the sick. At bottom, though he admired the royal generosity, Monsieur Vincent's heart was not in the scheme. The *Parlement* and the police were only concerned with public order which was their duty. Vincent de Paul considered that the poor man had his dignity and the beggar his freedom; he was an enemy of all constraint. Both Monsieur Vincent and Louise de Marillac preferred to rely upon persuasion: poor men, incapable of earning their own living, should be induced to shut themselves up voluntarily. Their almshouse of The Name of Jesus was a striking proof of the efficacy of their method, but the history of charitable organisation is full of the debate between order and liberty. Monsieur Vincent, otherwise so clear-sighted and practical, perhaps expected rather too much of human nature and the *mystique* of poverty. My own impression is that Louise de Marillac had not followed him very far along this road, and that she would have preferred to sacrifice liberty to order, in her desire to reduce suffering.

THE MYSTIQUE OF THE RULES

SINCE 1629 Louise de Marillac had been in the service of charity; since 1634 she had belonged to the society which she had founded (with Monsieur Vincent) for the practical work of charity. With her Daughters she had sought out poverty, sickness and misery in all its forms—in hospitals, among convicts, with the foundlings—and all with a prodigality of love which is simply astounding. But never for a moment did she forget that her first duty was to watch over the Congregation which was the instrument of all these benevolent works. To train and form her Daughters and to maintain their fervour—this was her primary responsibility if she were to ensure, for today and for tomorrow, the stability of their Congregation. She knew that a community founded on an idea is held upright by its Rule, as by a spinal column.

Vincent de Paul was never tired of emphasising the essential, the fundamental, notion of rule and of law. It is because it is established upon an unshakable system of laws that the vast and complex machine of the world revolves without pause. It was because the people of Israel had under their feet the religion of the Law that they were able to resist assaults which would, in the normal course of things, have destroyed them. Religious Orders, which are a permanent defiance of the world, continue to live despite the world, protected as they are by the armour of the Rule.

It is by no arbitrary inflation that we appeal in this way to such solemn truths in connection with the Rule of the Daughters of Charity. Their Rule summed up their existence and their being.

It was by the Rule that the Sisters lived in community, and by the Rule they were what they were. Every Christian must assuredly obey the law and the will of Christ: that is a generalised will which calls for an ordinary degree of obedience. But the religious who takes a vow of obedience goes beyond this everyday obedience. He has, as it were, alienated his own freewill and accepted the particular purposes of God, so that all his own acts are, fundamentally, acts of obedience. These particular purposes of God are manifest to the religious at every moment of the day by his Rule, which covers the whole of his external life and all his conscious acts. The mystic has bidden adieu to his own senses and his private judgment and abandons himself to God in love. The religious who has made his vow of obedience, by an analogous act which is also in part mystical, obeys his Rule without interposing his own personality: to obey is to love.

Since the Rule, as an expression of the particular purposes of God, is established on human experience, it is also keyed to the limits of what is possible to man and is adapted to his needs. While it binds and bends, compels and leads him, it also sustains him and gives him strong protection, leading him away from ways of temptation, and maintaining his powers of resistance in a state of alertness. His Rule is to him a luminous signal, sending from afar its warning of danger; it is to him a source of equilibrium and peace. As the Rule is the same for all, it guarantees unanimity, cohesion and harmony in the community, which includes among its members a diversity of personalities and a great variety of duties, all of which are controlled in detail by the Rule itself. Finally, the Rule provides a safeguard for human dignity because, although it absorbs a man, it has first been chosen and willed by him.

It was with this conception of the mystical value of the Rule that, as soon as it seemed to them that the Congregation was the will of God and would endure, Vincent de Paul and Mademoiselle applied themselves to giving the Daughters a Rule. In its earliest days, the community had lived by provisional regulations, each article of which was under

constant scrutiny in the light of experience. From this
experience there emerged the Rule, which had to be
sufficiently robust to ensure the perfection of the three vows,
yet sufficiently supple to be well adapted to the life of a
secular congregation of women, dedicated primarily to the
service of the sick and the poor. There must at many points
have been problems as to this equilibrium and many a conference between the two Founders, who were in hourly
contact with the manifold difficulties of their new venture.
The subject also occurs in their correspondence, although it
would arise more naturally in conversation following on a
study of the texts. Monsieur Vincent asked Louise to send
him outlines, which he would revise; or he himself draws up
up a synopsis and submits it to her for her advice. This she
would give candidly, with words of apology.

One point concerned her greatly. In the introductory
memorandum presented when the Rule was submitted for
approval, the Congregation was put under the sole authority
of the Archbishop of Paris, who could, upon the death of the
founder, appoint for the diocese any Superior he chose.
Louise was much afraid that in this total subordination to the
Archbishop there lay a certain danger:

'Permit me to say to your charity that the explanation
contained in our rules for the Daughters causes me to
desire for them the continued use of this title, which is
omitted, perhaps by accident, in the memorandum of
the terms of establishment. May not this condition, so
absolute, of dependence on Monseigneur, the Archbishop,
do us some harm in future years, since it gives liberty to
take us away from the direction of the Superior-General
of the Mission? Is it not necessary, Monsieur, that by
these articles of establishment your charity should be
given to us for a director in perpetuity? And these rules
which are to be given to us, is it the intention of Monseigneur that they are to be the ones indicated in the
text of the application? Does that require a separate

document, or may others be drawn up at will, since they are separately mentioned? In the name of God, Monsieur, do not allow anything to happen which might contribute in the smallest way to withdraw the direction of the Company from the hands in which God has placed it. For you may be assured that the Company would then no longer be what it is, and the sick poor would no longer be assisted, and thus I believe that the will of God would no longer be done among us.'

This was written in 1646. Monsieur Vincent turned a deaf ear and did not think it necessary to modify the text of the introductory memorandum. Louise de Marillac returned obstinately to the charge and in a more solemn tone, as though she were the instrument of a Divine warning.

'It seems to me that God put my soul in a great peace and simplicity, during the prayer that I made concerning the necessity that the Company of the Daughters of Charity should always be under the direction which Divine Providence has given to it, in spiritual as well as temporal matters. I think I have seen that it would be more to his glory that the Company should cease to function, rather than come under a change of direction, since it seems to me that this would be contrary to the will of God.

'The signs are that there is reason to believe that God has inspired, and made known from the beginning, his will for the perfecting of the works which his goodness wishes to perform. And you know, Monsieur, that in these beginnings it was suggested that the temporal control of the said Company, if it should fall vacant by mischance, should return to the Mission, by which it would be used for the teaching of country people.

'I hope that if your charity has understood of our Lord what I think he has told you in the person of St Peter that as it was upon that rock that he willed to build this Company, then it will persevere in the service our Lord asks, for the teaching of children and the consolation of the sick.'

This second request had no more effect than the first. Let us note in passing the dignity of the protagonists: each holds his ground. On November 26th, 1646, the Archbishop of Paris approved the rules of the Company in the text presented by Monsieur Vincent. The approbation was signed by the coadjutor, the Cardinal de Retz, in eulogistic terms, and the founder, Vincent de Paul, named Superior for life. There was great joy in Saint-Lazare and in the rue Saint-Denis. The Congregation now entered upon its lawful existence, securely founded on a canonical basis.

The joy was great, but not entirely unmixed. Louise certainly regretted that she had not obtained all the privileges she had requested, and it may be that, upon reflection, Monsieur Vincent shared her regret. These afterthoughts may provide the explanation for one rather curious circumstance: episcopal approbation was given on November 30th, 1646; yet Monsieur Vincent kept the fact a secret for no less than six months. His precise reason for delaying the announcement is unknown. It may be that he hoped to secure some modification of the text of the grant. Louise de Marillac became impatient and appraised him in a letter written in April, 1647, of the mounting expectancy in the community. This letter seems to have decided him, for on the 30th May, 1647, he communicated the approved text of the decree to the assembled community. We may say that this meeting was the completion and crown of that much smaller assembly, on July 31st, 1634, when Monsieur Vincent had read the first Regulations to Louise and a dozen 'Sisters'. On that day, the infant Company had promised obedience to a provisional Rule: the Congregation born of that obedience now engaged itself to a Rule which was definitive, as the Founder solemnly read the episcopal document to the Sisters, who knelt to hear it.

Like Moses when he brought the Law to Israel, Monsieur

Vincent pointed out that this Rule had come to them from God by the hands of his minister, and he renewed to the Daughters the blessings and cursings with which the earlier prophet had sealed his mission:

'My Daughters, I say to you what Moses said to the people of God. Here are rules which have been sent to you as from God himself. If you are faithful in keeping them, all the blessings of Heaven will descend upon you: you shall be blessed in your work and in your rest, blessed in what you do, and blessed in what you refrain from doing; and all things shall be filled with blessing by you.

'If—which God forbid!—any of you should not have this intention, I say to them what Moses said to those who would not obey the Law which he taught them as from God: you shall be cursed in the house, and cursed out of it; you shall be cursed in what you do, and in what you refrain from doing.

'I have already told you at other times, my Daughters, that he who gets into a ship to make a long voyage, must be submissive to all that is done in that ship. If he were not subject to all the ship's laws, which were made for his protection, he would be in danger of perishing. In the same way, those who are called by God to live in a holy community must observe all of its rules.

'I believe that each one of you is firmly resolved to keep the Rule. Are not all of you of the same mind?'

He then slowly read through the text of the Rule, bestowing on certain articles a word or two of veneration or gratitude. When he came to the passage which provided for the appointment of a new superior-general every third year, he interjected: 'That is, of course, when God shall have disposed of Mademoiselle.' As he spoke, Mademoiselle, on her knees like the rest, begged that no exception might be made; that rather her insufficiency and her poor health should be considered and she be relieved of the burden of command. Monsieur Vincent replied forthwith that the community would constantly pray for the restoration of her health, and that this would render her capable of doing the will of God. He then continued with the reading. When he had done, there ensued a moving dialogue between the Director and his Daughters:

'I believe that each one of you has firm intention of keeping the Rule. Are not all of you of this mind?'

The Sisters, listening upon their knees, answered, in voices which trembled with emotion, 'Yes, Father'.

Saint Vincent went on: 'I hope that his mercy will sustain your desires, by aiding you to accomplish what he asks of you. Do you give yourselves with all your hearts to him, my Daughters, to live by the observance of your holy Rule?'

'Yes, willingly.'

'Do you not desire with all your hearts to live and die in˙ it?'

'We do desire it.'

'I pray the sovereign goodness of God, that it may please him to pour out abundantly upon you every kind of grace and blessing, so that you may accomplish, perfectly and in all things, the good pleasure of his most holy will in the practice of your Rule.'

As though she had been provoked to the act by this solemn engagement, one of the Sisters now began to speak. She accused herself of frequent breaches of the Rule. Another Sister followed her example. As emotion reached its climax, Monsieur Vincent himself fell on his knees, and confessed that he also had often broken the Rule of the Mission; he was an unworthy servant, and had not the right to bless the Daughters; he would therefore call upon God to bless them himself. At these words, however, there was an outcry from the assembled Sisters, who refused to be deprived of the blessing of their Father. He allowed himself to be persuaded by their supplication, and gave his blessing to an assembly overcome by an emotion as of Pentecost.

We now come to describe a highly critical period in the

history of the congregation. The Church had approved the new institute and given it official recognition. But the documents which embodied the ecclesiastical Approbation had now to be submitted for the formal approval of the civil power—they had to be ratified by the *Parlement* of Paris. Here we come upon an obscure problem, on which historians of the Mission of the Daughters of Charity have not been very anxious to bring light to bear. They hesitate at this point, as if unwilling to know all the facts. We do not know them all. But what we do know, I set down here.

It will be recalled that Mademoiselle had not been altogether pleased with the terms of the Archbishop's Approbation, which did not altogether coincide with her objectives, nor, perhaps, with those of Vincent de Paul. Yet it was the text approved by their superiors and, as such, they accepted and revered it. While, therefore, the Founders were privately a little disappointed, they had no weighty reason for failing to open the necessary negotiations with the lawyers and this they proceeded to do. With the leisureliness observable in all administrations, the dossier, together with the King's Letters Patent, was remitted to the *Parlement*—by whose hands we do not know. It was probably handed to Meliand, the Procurator General.

Time passed. The *Parlement* was in no hurry. The community was up against an ingrained prejudice: nobody had ever heard of a congregation of women which was not cloistered, but which proposed to live a secular life based on a novel Rule. The *Parlement* was therefore insisting on making a careful study of the situation that would be created by this new institute—and the investigation would take up a good deal of time.

Years passed in exasperated negotiation. Then, in 1650, the name of Meliand was again mentioned in connection with the case. Now, Louise de Marillac was acquainted with this official, having consulted him at various times in connection with the *Enfants Trouvés*. She went to see him and gave an account of her visit in a somewhat curious letter to Monsieur Vincent.

'Yesterday I had occasion to see the Procurator-General, who did me the honour to receive me very courteously, and told me at once that I was there on a matter which happened to be in his own hands. I told him I was there only to refresh his memory. He asked me whether we claimed to be both regular and secular nuns. I gave him to understand that we claimed only the latter. He said to me that that was without precedent. I instanced to him the 'daughters' of Madame de Ville-neuve, and proved to him that they went about every-where. He assured me that our design was not dis-approved, and said much that was good of the Company, but that a matter of such importance needed to be care-fully considered. I testified to him my joy that he was interesting himself in the affair in this way, and begged him that, if the thing was without merit, or if it should be a long drawn-out affair, he should destroy it entirely, but that if it was good, we earnestly begged him to establish it firmly, and that we had put this way of life to the test for at least a dozen or fifteen years, during which time, by the grace of God, all had gone well without trouble. He said to me: "Let me think about it, I do not say for months, but for several weeks"; he took the trouble to see us to the carriage; he was in the courtyard; and he showed us great goodwill, charged us to greet you very humbly, saying he would be but a usurer if he received the very humble thanks we paid him for the honour he did to all our Sisters, when they ventured to approach him in their needs, which were as much for the poor convicts as for the little children.'

We note in this letter the casual statement that she 'had occasion', for all the world as though she were unconcerned to know what had become of a certain dossier which closely concerned her. We observe further that, according to the

description by Louise, Meliand made no allusion to the
dossier, but conducted himself in a detached manner, as
though the papers were not in his possession. And indeed, if
he *had* had them, he would have known from the approved
text what was the precise situation in religion of Mademoiselle's Daughters and would have had no need to interrogate
her upon the point.

Meliand died. He was succeeded by Fouquet, who wished
to reopen the question (at whose request?), made a search
for the dossier—and could not find it. It was lost. Somewhere,
in the offices of the Procurator-General or at Saint-Lazare or
in the rue Saint-Denis or at some point on the road from
Saint-Lazare to the *Parlement* the dossier had vanished. When
the new Procurator-General informed them that he was
unable to find the papers, Vincent de Paul and Louise made
a search in every likely place, but without result. On
November 25th, 1651, Louise wrote Vincent de Paul:

> 'I have not found a single paper relating to the estab-
> lishment, and I recall that one day your charity took the
> trouble to give us a reading from the petition which you
> had presented to Monseigneur of Paris, with our Rule
> following; and thinking that it ought to remain with us,
> I asked you for it. I believe that the reason why we did
> not retain it in our possession was that there was still some
> piece of business outstanding.'

Louise went on to write as though she saw in this untoward
event a sort of visitation for her own shortcomings and sins.
She ended her letter by saying that she was sending a text
which she had put together from her recollection of the public
reading given in 1647. Finally, as though she feared that her
remarks might be lacking in clarity, she added a postscript
which, so far from enlightening us, confuses the issue still
further:

> 'I believe that Brother Ducourneau would know where
> to find both the original and the copy of the petition

which was presented, together with the act of establishment, which it seems to me we never had.'

All that clearly emerges is that the dossier had gone astray and that none of the interested parties knew where or how it had been lost. It now became necessary to draw up another text and the Founders addressed themselves to this work of authorship as to a quite new task, as though there were no such thing as a copy or draft of the text of 1646. This time either Louise de Marillac was more persuasive, or else Monsieur Vincent conceded that she had been in the right, for the new text provided that the Daughters of Charity should remain always under the direction of the Superior-General of the Mission. Louise de Marillac may have been obstinate, but her foresight had been clear: she had preserved the unity of a congregation which, destined to spread over the entire world, would inevitably have split into autonomous fragments for want of a recognised centre and head to preserve intact the spirit of the society. Quite simply, she had preserved the identity of the Daughters of Charity.

Definitely approved in 1655, the documents of the constitution and Rule were forwarded to Rome by the efforts of Anne of Austria herself. They were finally ratified by the *Parlement* in 1658. Twenty-five years had been needed to provide the congregation with a Rule—which stresses the vital significance of this Rule. Vincent de Paul had promulgated the definitive text in the general meeting on August 8th, 1655. For his Daughters, this was the same text as they had received with such enthusiasm in 1647; they solemnly renewed their submission. Then Mademoiselle, and after her all the Sisters present, affixed their signatures to this charter of the Congregation, any who could not write signing with a cross. Monsieur Vincent signed last and then were added the names of the absent. The Pope, the King, the Archbishop of Paris, the *Parlement*, Vincent de Paul, Louise de Marillac and the Daughters of Charity, all were

in accord as to a contract which was to govern the new
foundation for centuries to come.

Founder and Foundress made it a duty to expound the
Charter, so as to determine its meaning and its spirit.
Vincent de Paul based upon it the whole programme of his
discourses from the year 1655 to the time of his death.
Neither his ever-increasing work, nor his frequent illnesses,
were ever allowed to divert him from this task.

In two conferences given in August 1650, the Founder laid
down the principle of obedience to the Rule, according to his
'little method', which consists, first, of considering the reasons
one may have for obeying a command, then the fault one
may commit by deficient obedience and finally the means at
one's disposal to ensure perfect obedience. The first conference is a dialogue in which the Sisters discover for themselves, under his guidance, the reasons they have for observing the Rule and the faults they commit when they fail to
keep it well. The second is a proper conference in which he
expounds his own 'little thoughts'. The rules are of God.
They have been given to the Daughters not to restrict them,
but to sustain them.

'As the birds have wings to fly, but do not find they
are weighed down by them, so the Daughters of Charity
have their Rule, which serves them as wings to fly to
God; and very far from being weighed down, they fly
easily when they are in good training.'

His explanation is rich in supernatural perception and in
fervour. The aim of the Daughters of Charity is to honour
the charity of our Lord and thus to give joy to God. Yes,
God does rejoice when he sees you imitate the charity of his
Son. To give joy to God—what a vocation that is! The
tendency of the Rule is to make you into saints, to make you
share in the Spirit of God! From poor girls to sharers in the
spirit of God! It is in serving the sick poor that the Daughters
have a share in the Spirit of God, and give joy to him. So
the service of the sick takes precedence of everything else.

To serve the sick you will, if necessary, leave everything, even prayer, even Sunday Mass, though it be an obligation; that is what we call leaving God in order to find him.

Happy are you, to have entered a Company with so exalted an aim! And as though moved by a spirit of prophecy, Monsieur Vincent concluded:

'If you are faithful in the keeping of your Rule, God will do through your Company such things as have never been heard of.'

This conference was given on July 21st, 1658. Louise, when she heard those striking and emphatic words, had reached a point when she began to know that her end was near and that her own life's work was done. She must have experienced profound emotion. Now she comprehended this Rule, which had caused her such anxiety, as a sort of mystic bond uniting the wills of her Daughters. Her work, and Vincent's work, most intimately combined, were truly the work of God.

PART IV

THE INTERIOR LIFE OF LOUISE DE MARILLAC

THE SOUL MISTRESS OF THE BODY

To REMARK that a great change took place in Louise de Marillac between 1645 and 1650 would be merely naïve; for the passage of time stills tempests in us all and slows the pace of life. Louise had exposed herself fully to the wear-and-tear of life and she was glad of the tranquility.

A transformation was at work in her as though she were now gathering all her strength for a new ascent towards a richer and deeper life. To assist us in following her itinerary we have no other guide than Louise herself, in a few sparse letters and odd notes which are but rarely dated.

Louise de Marillac had now arrived at a time when she could lay down some of her burdens, when she could be relieved of those heavy cares which had so agitated her mind and torn her heart. Her son had at last found an occupation and was married. The houses of the Daughters of Charity were well established and organised, her Daughters firm in their religious state. The *Enfants Trouvés*, which had all but foundered in the hurricane of the civil wars, had picked up and was now advancing steadily towards stability.

These intimate letters have been edited for the private use of the two Vincentian congregations. The editors have not attempted—or have not found it possible—to establish any great precision in chronology, but they have been able to convey that a far-reaching spiritual re-orientation was taking place in Mademoiselle and to justify a provisional grouping of the letters into the period before and the period after 1650. This date will provide us with our signpost.

Everywhere she could see the hand of Providence, gently leading men and their affairs to a point of equilibrium, which she herself hoped to reach before she died. She could retreat now into her inner room, whence so many claims had drawn her forth, and pay a little attention to her soul.

Let us pause a moment to look again at her portrait. We might suppose that the artist had taken licence and effaced from her features the wrinkles and furrows engraved upon it by her many sorrows. But we have the discreet testimony of her own Daughters that her countenance retained its charm to the end. No matter what hour of day she might be disturbed, her visitor was invariably received with the same smile. 'When we were ill', they said, 'she would come to see us, and it seemed to us that her visit healed us. If she had occasion to reproach us, we knew that her rebuke was just.'

Louise had great powers of persuasion and knew how to get what she wanted. Her charm doubtless sprang from a natural gift of grace, from a certain accessibility of soul. It sprang too from her will to give pleasure and be of use, and therefore from a domination of herself and her humours. This self-mastery was not inborn self-control, placid and cool, but acquired by a strong effort of charity.

First, she was completely mistress of her body, and this was a great merit in her. Her body had given her a great deal of trouble. She suffered from a chronic malady which was apparently some kind of nervous gastritis, which would throw her into sudden fevers, diagnosed—as was usual then with most feverish illnesses—as either tertiary or quartern ague. She could take only a little food while the attacks lasted and weakness compelled her to stay in bed. She was extraordinarily sensitive to cold, and especially to the 'bise', that searching wind from the north-east which often blows through the winter and the spring, attacking the face and neck in particular. When she was about fifty she had wanted to wear the habit of her Daughters, covering her head with the simple peasant cowl. But so bitter were her headaches that she was forced to revert to the fashionable veiled head-dress of the great ladies, which is now the normal headgear of her order. Like all feverish patients, she had a firm belief in remedies, discreet and otherwise, some of which she prepared for herself, bestowing them also with the greatest liberality upon Monsieur Vincent and the priests of the Mission. She was a devotee of the medical profession and readily left one doctor for another if she thought the new one would serve her better. We need not call this a weakness: only the robust in health can afford to despise healers and remedies.

In 1647, when she asked to be allowed to resign from the Congregation on grounds of health, Monsieur Vincent remarked with a smile that she had already been at death's door for ten whole years and was only kept alive by a miracle, and that everyone would beg God to keep up the miracle indefinitely. Eight years later she renewed the request on the same grounds. Vincent de Paul retorted in the same terms, changing only the number of years from ten to twenty. There may be some verbal exaggeration in the anecdote, but the fact remains that her life was broken up by spells of illness which were to some extent shortened by will-power, and from which she promptly returned to her duties among her Daughters.

Her administrative work called for much time and for a nimble mind. In a letter to a Daughter, she remarked that it had just struck ten, that she ought to have been in bed long ago, but was still writing. All the powers of her mind had to be constantly available for a multitude of tasks: to direct the sisters in their work, encourage and console them, and manage the scattered houses of the institute. She excelled in the professional work of a 'housekeeper-in-chief' who has to put a good face on things with very little money. Monsieur Vincent marvelled, in 1655, that she was so skilful a manager, He did not know, he said, of any religious house that was better conducted than hers. All the houses he knew had had debts and difficulties, while the Daughters, thanks to the prudent management of Mademoiselle, had no debts, even

F

though they had lately had to build and to fulfil many obligations.

This gift for management is a rare and valuable one. It calls for a precise knowledge of commodities and constant retrenchment wherever a saving can be made. Mademoiselle received the most eminent ladies in the kingdom and paid her respects to them in their elegant homes; she was always decently, if poorly, dressed, out of fidelity to her vows. One day Monsieur Vincent, reproached in the Council of Conscience with the poverty of his clothes, replied with a smile: 'No hole, no patch!' Mademoiselle could have said the same. Her deputies, wanting to see her finely dressed, brought her one day a good piece of serge to make a cloak; she put it carefully away in a cupboard, to save for some urgent need. When her son's clothes could no longer be worn in public by one in his position, Mademoiselle would look them over with care and bestow them on one of her vaga-bonds. These trivial details shine with the dignity of charity and of evangelical poverty, and they have besides their economic significance. The careful superior of a community, saving up bits and pieces of cloth and thread when her work was done, to use them again, because it is a penance to work with short thread, and because, if the scraps are used, the box will never be empty—such a one had well learned the lesson of poverty.

Notice in Louise de Marillac, as in her director, the con-stant use of diminutives. In the eyes of the Founders all they handled and all they did was 'little'. With Vincent de Paul, this mode of thought was so habitual that when he wanted to grumble about his chronic malady, a form of malaria, he was accustomed to say that 'his little fevers were a little prolonged'. When the Founders gave their opinion, they expressed their 'little thoughts'. It is interesting to observe how all this—and we could find many examples—is far from narrow-spirited or petty. It is the mark of a refinement of mind which can wait for favourable opportunities to make its full effect felt, and hold something in reserve for use when wanted—'for the encounter', as they said in those days.

In Louise, this natural refinement had been developed by her wide and varied culture. She was well acquainted with Latin, and had a taste for philosophy and theology. She had read substantial books, such as the *Imitation of Christ*, Luis of Granada, and the works of Francis de Sales. She had studied the Bible. She had a feeling for the fine arts—and indeed more than a feeling, since her pictures have a professional touch. This organiser was also a humanist, an intellectual and an artist. She had no occasion to display the riches of her mind in the letters she wrote, for her correspondents were usually uneducated girls. It is from the letters she received that we can form an opinion. Michel de Marillac, her father's brother, treats Louise as his intellectual equal and as a philosopher, with a settled habit of reflection. Camus was pleased that he could keep up with her a taste for psychology, a difficult study for a woman in the seventeenth century. In the years between 1630 and 1660, when she counted among her friends many society women, she breathed easily in the atmosphere of the *salon* and the literary world, though she was very far from sharing its interests. In her manner of writing there is not a trace of preciousness; but we observe an instinctive and methodical preference for exact thinking, for the word which best expresses the idea, for the noble and plain phrase. She adopted a clear and exact syntax and wrote in correct French. The style of Montaigne was still loaded with archaisms; even Francis de Sales is not always free from them. But Louise wrote a very deliberate French in the style of the educated ladies of her day, the style of a lady of refinement and not of a pedant.

In her search for the truth she was always very much a woman. By this I do not mean to imply that she used subtlety in either thought or action. I mean that she was always careful, in the manner of refined women, to please, to conciliate and to persuade. She could use the word that caresses, the turn of phrase that sets her reader at ease. A Daughter reading a letter from Mademoiselle was made to feel that she herself was, at that moment, Louise de Marillac's only care. So reproach could be accepted without any bitterness. We can savour the charm of this feminine style of writing in a letter written to Vincent de Paul. She knows he is very busy and that she is very importunate, but she wants something from him, and this is how she writes:

'May I appear before you as a poor suppliant, and beg you, for the love of God, to grant me the charitable alms of a little visit? I am in great need of this, since I am not able to send the matter to you, but it is hindering me from doing many things, and so I am obliged to trouble you.

P.S. If your charity could come today.'

Observe the imperative postscript, the work of a woman who has already gained her point and only needs to press her victory home. There is another letter to Monsieur Vincent which ends with the words: 'Do you know that I am the littlest of your Daughters?' She knows very well that Vincent de Paul would be touched by that avowal.

She was very much a woman even in her faults, and for these we do not have to search, for she herself tells us with great simplicity what they were.

On one occasion, she was distracted. There had been a misunderstanding with the Abbé de Vaux. Her nephew should have kept an appointment with the Abbé, but this had been broken because Louise herself had failed to write a letter, which she had promised to do:

'I am often taken by surprise in this way, because I am little used to conversation. Before God, I am ashamed of this, because I do not make use of my freedom in the world to be more with him. This is one of my greatest faults, and I tell you the truth concerning it.'

We may see what is the fault to which she refers. Her mind is of a serious cast, and it attaches but little weight to words exchanged with persons in the world, even though to the world they are important. So it came about that she forgot them, or seemed to regard them as of no consequence, and sensitive people were offended and hurt. Louise was distracted: for she lived in a whole world of activity, thought and feeling, cut off from that everyday world of triviality in which she none the less had to live.

She was also very quick of tongue. On this point, all who knew her were in agreement. Vincent de Paul, the Ladies, the Daughters, all spoke of her quickness of tongue. She herself acknowledged it and accused herself of it. I do not mean a capacity for quick decisions, which is characteristic of any leader. I mean her sharp reaction to error or fault or cross-grained action. A reaction expressed and exhausted in a word, in a gesture; but one which disturbs others profoundly and with lasting result. Louise once answered sharply one of her Daughters who had wounded her by some impertinence, and the next instant begged pardon for the rebuke. As we have seen, she was prostrated by the behaviour of her son and so great was her agitation that she was completely shaken and lost consciousness. At bottom she was a woman of passionate disposition, who had suppressed both her inclinations and her imagination, just as she had mastered the deficiencies of her body. But she was dealing with a strong adversary and sometimes her passions revolted: Louise was a Marillac to the very end.

HER REAL LIFE AN INTERIOR ONE

ON THE DAY following the death of Louise de Marillac, during the moving scene in which Vincent de Paul addressed her Daughters on the subject of her virtues, one of the Sisters remarked that Mademoiselle had been an interior soul. To all appearance she had lived in the external world, in a great round of activity and administration. She was obliged to see many people, write a great many letters, and go into the details of many practical matters. But by a natural reaction she was able to withdraw into herself the instant she was at liberty and her frequent retreats into her 'interior castle' sufficed to maintain there a constant spiritual life even when she was not conscious of it. This aptitude was a gift of nature. She said herself that from her early youth she had had a great facility in meditation, which in the end became a faculty of, and a need for, analysis. Where almost all of us experience a real difficulty in self-scrutiny and in self-examination, she was always turning to her own interior spiritual world as to a refuge. This is perhaps the tendency which she so simply described as the true sense of 'being distracted'.

Within this refuge she found God and herself—herself in the presence of God. From this encounter flowed her prayer, her joys, her anxieties. Here was the source of her humility. We must study this without preconceived ideas. Her humility was less given than Saint Vincent de Paul's to overstrained expressions and measured gestures, yet it was just as profound. She fills us with astonishment. She declared that she was a sinner, that she had a hundred times merited Hell, that through her own fault the community was decadent and in peril of death, as a punishment for her sins. When she wrote to her director, there flowed from her pen the most violent self-accusations of crime and abominable disorder. She would throw herself on her knees before her Daughters, begging them to pardon her the scandal she was causing them. She would stretch herself upon the floor of the refectory and invite the Daughters to tread her underfoot. And the person who spoke and acted in this way was clear of vision, passionate for the truth, penetrating in her self-scrutiny. Was she, then, in error concerning herself? Was she in truth a miserable sinner, or are we to believe that her spiritual reading had in it too much misuse of affective language and that she had formed a habit of using conventional language which was too strong for the purpose, when all she desired was to set in relief her regret that since her soul was not sinless, her love of God was less than perfect? She was too honest and too truthful to use language to disguise her thought. What she said was what was in her mind.

Our inability to conceive of this degree of humility arises in part from the fact that we unconsciously judge according to our own standards, and that, though not exactly drunk with self-esteem, we have some difficulty in despising ourselves by comparing ourselves with others whose deficiencies we feel or suspect. But Louise never compared herself with others. Since she lived continually in the presence of God, it was with him that she compared herself. She was confounded by the absurdity of her nothingness before the Divine Being; confounded also by the gravity of the least of her sins, which since they were directed at God, should be multiplied to infinity. Her practice of the interior life, of meditation and prayer, gave to these things a violent, burning reality, which provoked expressions every bit as burning and violent as the sins, which no words can fittingly describe.

When professional psychologists undertake to solve the problem of the humility of the saints, they merely make it more complicated. We may agree with them that psychoanalysis reveals, in the depth of being, a cauldron from which any and every fever may rise. But if this psychology is scientifically concerned to be objective and complete, it must recognise in those same depths a divine mystery which is an antidote to fevers and poisons. Our being is the theatre of an unceasing conflict, in which we are at once actors and onlookers. To suppress God before the fight begins and to yield the victory to malign powers, is to mutilate nature by suppressing a problem which we claim to be solving.

Now for some of the saints the real drama lies here. At some hour of their life, a life very possibly both pure and fervent, they have experienced an earthquake of the soul, have lost the feeling for God, the feeling of the presence of God, and all faith in his existence. Louise de Marillac and Vincent de Paul both made formal declaration that, for days in the one case, for months in the other, the vacuum was complete and God was totally absent. They were in a kind of Hell, of which they saw both top and bottom—God and the anti-thesis of God. They felt the gravity of sin more sharply than do the sinners who commit it in seeking their own interest and pleasure. They could remember, and being conscious of some semblance of sin in themselves, the memory burned and consumed them. Hence the use of vivid expressions of horror—expressions which sound affected and are simply realistic. Louise de Marillac was most truly sincere and lucid when she humiliated herself in her nothingness and accused herself of sin. Her humility was an experience.

She meditated on this experimental humility and since she had a very uncommon gift of introspection she saw clearly that it was not sufficient to have plumbed the depths of her nothingness in order to have a horror of it in the presence of God. True humility is a supernatural virtue, a free gift of God, by which it is given to us to see that God is all and we ourselves are nothing. This is what she said to M. de Vaux, speaking with much freedom, because she felt that she was understood by a man of great virtue and wide culture:

'Since you ask me, I will tell you very simply that it is

necessary to wait in peace until grace shall produce in us true humility; giving us an understanding of our power-lessness, humility causes us to suffer from what you have called slight infirmities, pride, sensitivity, without the hope that all those things can be destroyed in us, who are, and who will be all our lives, tossed about by such agitations.'

In one sense, sin is always present in us. With her usual liveliness, she expressed this idea as follows: 'Even after confession, it seemed to me that sin remained in my soul.' This is more than a memory, it is a root, an ever-present possibility which must cause us to tremble and maintain us in a state of humility. At the same time, this woman of direct commonsense, the contemporary of Pascal, having overthrown man, proceeds to set him on his feet again:

'While the power to commit sin is gravely damaging to the soul, it is none the less a mark of its excellence, and cannot be quite useless to the soul, since God does not withhold the grace which is necessary to abstain from it.'

When she had thus measured the gravity of sin, its permanence, and human responsibility for its permanence, the bitterness and the greatness of the combat of life, it is not astonishing that she should have struggled with sin with a relentlessness which, to our superficial minds, seems to spring from an obsession. Monsieur Vincent said of Louise that in her confessions she plucked herself clean, going in pursuit of her slightest fault and weeping for it with such grief and tears that it was scarcely possible to comfort her. Perhaps this was morbid sensitivity, but it is evidence of an exception-ally clear view of the greatness of God and the misery of man.

The faults which gave rise to this grievous contrition were light. Monsieur Vincent, a priest of the utmost discretion in every respect, above all in things like this, once felt obliged to demand boldly, in the presence of the assembled Sisters: 'What [wrong] have you ever seen in her, in the thirty-eight years you have known her? What have you seen

in her? A few little gnats and midges of imperfection but
mortal sin—oh, never!'

To Louise, standing in the presence of God, these gnats
seemed monsters. She held herself responsible for their continued presence, and punished herself because they were
there. Her asceticism was not meant to achieve mastery
over her own flesh—which stood much more in need of the
gentleness one shows to the poor. No. Her object was
punishment. Guilt must be punished with the hair shirt and
the discipline. Her director forbade nothing that seemed to
be inspired by the love of God; but he restrained his penitent
when excess might well become a temptation to pride and
endanger her health, which was always delicate and
essential in the work she was doing. He allowed her the use of
a cincture of small silver roses, which he had on loan from
Mlle Du Fay, and advised her to use it instead of the shirt of
horsehair, which might overheat the blood.

She set death within this perspective of merited punishment. We are prisoners, sentenced to death, justly sentenced,
for sin has merited death. To accept the justness of our dying
is an act of good sense which already serves as a counterweight to sin itself.

All sorrow and suffering serves as a counterweight to sin,
though in a different sense. Louise felt convinced that she
was called, from birth, to sorrow and suffering. God desired
her to go to him by way of the Cross since her life had known
not a single day without sorrow. Obviously she didn't mean
just physical suffering, from which she did feel relief, but
also her constant moral anguish. This was her lot and she
accepted her cross, embracing it willingly; through it she
entered her 'private cloister'. She took with both hands the
chalice of sorrow which was offered to her and drained it to
the last drop. I do not find that she paid any special attention,
as some saints have done, to the redemptive nature of suffering; she took it and embraced it for herself, that she might be
likened to Christ in his sufferings; that she might be united

with him, love him (since to love and to suffer are the same thing), love him above all, and be one with him in his for-sakenness. This imitation of Christ, this resolve to reproduce in her human measure the conditions of our Lord's incarnate Life, is in fact the supreme law written once for all upon her earthly road, to stay with her in all her ways.

If the stress of sorrow was occasionally relaxed, leaving intervals of dryness, these were filled with scruples, those timid but tenacious camp-followers of sorrow. Frequent as the deadly fogs of the seventeenth century, they were the inevitable malady of sedentary people given to analysis and reflection. They are the shadows of the interior life, and no man knows whence they come. Sister Cecilia may love God, but one cheerless morning she will persuade herself that her love is not returned; the idea takes firm root, grows, spreads, and destroys her. Sister Marie forms the notion that she is too much attached to her confessor; she must make a change, or she will be in peril of losing her soul; whereas Sister Louise feels that this same confessor detests her, is quite unable to understand her and is unworthy of her confidence. Thus the confessor is, without knowing it, the accidental cause of a double drama. These are but three examples: scruples are as varied as temperaments. They range from the simple 'gnat', which will take flight if you breathe on it, to the monster which digs itself in and feeds on blood.

Louise de Marillac, when dealing with the subject of scruples, gave her Daughters so much counsel and in such detail that it is easy to see that she herself had had much experience of the trouble. In her correspondence with her director, this is the subject of discreet but continuous com-plaint. She always needs a full quarter-of-an-hour to discuss her scruple: she would be lost without remedy if a hearing were to be refused. And it was so until the very end. She never succeeded in extricating herself from this flank attack of the invisible enemy, even when, caressed by the Spirit in the citadel, she had driven the foe to the outworks of her soul. She was never free from surprise attacks; ill-defended, she was very often overshadowed by light fears and afflictions, which her director reproached in her as ingratitude to God who bestowed on her very special attractions to himself.

We may perceive these movements of flux and reflux throughout her correspondence and her retreat notes. What we have on this subject is a little too precise and schematic for modern taste. She generally made two retreats a year and would have made many more, had not her director restrained her within these prudent limits. One of these retreats was always arranged for Pentecost, in celebration of the great liberating grace of 1623. Several of these pentecostal retreats had, as we shall see, a decisive effect on her progress towards holiness.

The framework of her retreats is strictly classical, divided according to the stages of the spiritual life through which she passed rapidly, using, for her spiritual reading, especially Luis of Granada's *Guide* and the *Devout Life* of Francis de Sales. These books hold the attention of the mind and prevent it from wandering, without restricting the liberty of love. A rapid note here and there allows us to record the movements of her heart. I shall return to this point.

Exercised by sorrow and disturbed by contradictory forces, the dogmas and gifts of religious experience were gradually clarified by prayer, and by her efforts on the road towards holiness; while the meditations and graces of every day contributed ever more abundantly to the building up of her original spiritual personality.

HER PRAYER

AFTER A CERTAIN date the interior life of Louise de Marillac consisted of nothing but prayer. Verbal prayer had always occupied an important place in her life. The confraternities to which she belonged, and the particular devotions she undertook, imposed upon her the recital of long offices, such as those thirty-three daily acts of devotion by which she commemorated the years of our Lord's life on earth. These prayers formed part of the universal prayer of adoration which is due to God from his creatures. But they were just as much a way of giving expression to the overflowing abundance of her life, which circumstances had forced her to bottle up within herself; whenever she had sought to break her bonds, something had gone awry. Her prayer is therefore one way, and perhaps the best way, of getting to know her.

Her prayer was never sentimental. Love, of course, animated it, but love restrained in its manifestations by humility, as though it were astonished that it had the audacity to show itself. Her prayer is fairly intellectual, seeking as it advances new foundations in doctrine. It is theological, which may seem surprising in a woman, but it need no longer astonish us when we recall her love of philosophy and the scriptures, rare gifts even among the devout of those days. Her prayer is obviously saturated in the Scriptures, and especially of the Gospels, which impart to it a special resonance, different even from that of Monsieur Vincent, which runs in a more familiar vein and springs more immediately from his daily activities and needs.

She addresses her prayer spontaneously to the Trinity. When she begs for a spirit of unity in the members of her Congregation, she does so in the name and image of the unity of the Most Holy Trinity, to which all things must return since all things have their source there. Man is made in the image of the Trinity: he is threefold by virtue of his memory, his intelligence and his will. It is interesting to notice this Augustinian attitude in Louise and to note the importance she gives to memory, which is the reservoir from which we draw the materials of prayer, which we always bring to an end by invoking the Trinity, Father, Son and Holy Ghost.

The movement of admiration and love which the mystery of the Resurrection inspired in her is an original feature of her devotion which I have not encountered in other spiritual writers. What exchanges of love, what effusions must have taken place between Father and Son on Easter morning, when, having shown himself to Mary Magdalen, the Son appeared before the Father. We recall the great phrase of St Augustine: 'We will know only in heaven with what fulness the Son this day dwells with his Father.' The intimate life of the three Divine Persons is the great source of our Paschal joy, which is genuine in proportion as our joy is associated with the joy of the Trinity.

I have given the example of the Resurrection. Louise's prayer follows the rhythm of the liturgy, and here again she is theological, since the liturgy is the visible face of theology.

Her prayer increased in intensity with the beginning of Lent, when in the feastings of Mardi Gras men seemed to lose their reason. Her fervour deepened also in Passiontide, as she lived through the sorrow of our Lord. She prayed to Christ tormented throughout the night of his agony, in the strictly theological statement: 'You suffered as Man because you were offended as God.' Pilate, knowing him to be innocent, condemned him through self-interest, the most insidious of temptations. 'I beg God for the grace to be entirely delivered from this temptation, and never for any consideration let me be separated from justice.' The Good Thief was certainly a criminal with a great many misdeeds upon his conscience, but it sufficed that he should turn his heart to God for him to gain Paradise: 'My Jesus, how easy it is to win you!'

Jesus cried out with thirst, but willed not to quench it: 'You willed to die without any quenching of your thirst, to show us that after your death you would always be athirst for our deliverance.'

Mary, on Calvary, said 'Yes' to the Crucifixion, just as she did to the Incarnation. 'You desired that Mary should acquiesce in your death, which was in a sense a tearing asunder, as though you were no longer her Son.'

The prayer of Jesus Crucified rose spontaneously from her heart: 'I no longer desire anything but to be the subject of this despised King. O Cross, how much you are to be loved! I take refuge in you as in my cloister!' This taste for the retired and hidden life, which she had always had, joined the Blood of the Redemption with the radiance of the Annunciation, and with the hidden life of Jesus in the womb of his Mother. The Feast of the Annunciation occurs about the time of Easter, and is not to be separated from it.

This is a feast which, in her life and the early years of her community, marked some very important stages. She returned to this festival again and again, by a natural inclination of her heart, to adore the Infant Jesus in his hidden life. If it is the mystic who speaks here, we note that this is a mother who has known the joys of maternity, and her voice carries inflexions of genuine tenderness. She says to Mary: 'You were happy because at least for that hour, he was entirely your own.' And to Jesus she said, as to a familiar Friend: 'What were you doing while you were in her womb, little Child? And what secrets did you reveal to her?' Here is a thought which opens up the way to a 'Berullian' meditation which might indeed lead the fervent soul far along the road to contemplation. But Louise, a woman 'lost and absorbed in truth and justice', as she herself said, could never allow herself to be led away by tenderness in prayer, and at the height of her fervour and desire for the hidden life she made this declaration: 'It is true that I would prefer to appear no more to human eyes, but should I not in such a case be afraid, that I had escaped from sight in order to be the more esteemed?' It was always thus with her: her eyes were raised to heaven, but her feet were on the earth.

Sometimes in her prayers she had moments of elation, moments when she stood on the summit, as she put it. She also had her moments of dryness, and of calm level going. There were other moments when she came down from the heights of theology to take refuge in that secret life of hers, like a little girl. Here were memories of her troubled childhood—or is it that each of us has a private corner of the mind, where both great and small become again like a little child?

She had prayers of her own composition, original and long, to which she adhered because they were not common property. These she said a fixed number of times and she could not do without them. Monsieur Vincent disapproved this habit, not because the prayers were not correct, but because he held that no one should load himself with unnecessary obligations, formulas or practices. Such things fatigue the soul, and take up time which ought to be given to work or sleep. He ordered his penitent to lay aside these superfluous prayers, but she set such a value on them that he had to allow her to say them in times of anxiety, as, for example, when her son was ill. In one of her letters she admits that she has preferences of this kind:

'I think I should also say to your charity that I once had, and still do have, a certain amount of sorrow that I must leave out these little prayers. My thought was, that the Holy Virgin desired me to do her this little service of gratitude, and that I should find comfort with her by telling her of the things which hinder me, with the resolve to please her in some other way, and to serve her with more fervour; but that my resolutions are feebly carried out, and often neglected.

'Help me, of your charity, and give me your blessing often, and present me to God, all unworthy as I am, as a good father does with his prodigal children, for you well know that is what I am, and that I am, my much honoured Father, your very obedient servant.'

She had another private prayer, and this was most secret, for it was locked up in a casket which was not to be opened till after her death. This was a specially-blessed rosary which she never omitted to say throughout her life. Of this rosary she had several copies made, until there was one for each of her Sisters.

'The little rosary is the one which three years ago I asked permission of your charity to say for my private intentions. I have in a casket a number of these rosaries, with some thoughts on the subject written down, to be left to all my Sisters after my death, if your charity permits. None of the Sisters knows anything about it. This rosary is in honour of the hidden life of our Saviour in his state of imprisonment in the womb of his Mother, to congratulate her on her happiness during those nine months; and the three little grains are to honour her by her three wonderful titles of Daughter of the Father, Mother of the Son, and Bride of the Holy Ghost. That is the principle of this little devotion, which by the grace of God, all unworthy as I am, I have never discontinued, since the time indicated, and which I hope to carry out in full, by the aid of the same grace of God, if your charity so commands. And this little exercise, in my intention, is to ask of God, by the Incarnation of his Son and the prayers of the Holy Virgin, the purity necessary to the Company of the Sisters of Charity, and the stability of the said Company, according to his good pleasure.'

We do not find that Monsieur Vincent paid any attention to this chaplet as there is no further mention of it in the correspondence.

It is necessary to mention these subsidiary devotions because they allow us to enter into familiar communion with Louise de Marillac. But they are far from characteristic of her prayer, which is anchored to more solid things: to the will of God, as manifested to her at each moment in the Rule; to God's Providence, which protects her at every moment, keeping at a distance every danger, as on that memorable day when the floor collapsed, and which shows itself the whole time in all the houses of the institute, in all sorts of ways which could never be publicly known, but which her heart stores up with careful love.

Let us pause a moment to consider some of her 'summits', which mark her out among the spiritual leaders of her time. Not all of the theologians contemporary with her held the belief in the Immaculate Conception, and devotion to our Lady at that time did not stress this mystery. But Louise de Marillac returned to it again and again, and founded all her thoughts about Mary on it. She said herself, with more brevity than we could wish, that she had meditated on the subject before the Christmas crib, and that she was sorry her mind was not capable of showing the world the beautiful things God had let her see. She goes on to say that the Immaculate Conception was strictly not so much a miraculous privilege as an act of justice, since by the Incarnation Mary consented to become the Mother of God. Her Immaculate Conception had far-reaching consequences for Mary's consciousness, from which was excluded that instinct for sin which afflicts us all; for her judgment, which was always upright and sound; and for her will, which was always strong. We have to admire the tone of this reasoned meditation, which passes from the traditional doctrine of preservation from original sin to a generalisation, almost modern in tone, which links up the mystery of Mary Immaculate with the concepts of thinking and judgment.

It was to this pure source that Louise desired to attach her Congregation, which could become the first religious society consecrated to the Immaculate Conception of Mary. On December 7th, 1658, she asked Vincent de Paul so to dedicate her community during the Mass of the feast day,

which he joyfully consented to do. Mademoiselle composed
the Act of Consecration, and read it in the name of all her
Daughters. In it, she declared that the community took Mary
Immaculate as the sole Mother of the Congregation, and
gave itself to her irrevocably.

December 8th, 1658, is a date of particular splendour in
the spiritual history of the Congregation. Every year the
Act of Consecration, first read by the Foundress, is read and
ratified. The Act therefore has its place in the history of the
dogma, which, by way of the Miraculous Medal, gradually
developed to its culmination with the solemn Definition, and
the reply of the Virgin herself at Lourdes: 'I am the Immaculate Conception.'

Still more important in the Foundress's prayer was her
devotion to the Holy Spirit. This had its basis in an attitude
of her mind, which was constantly leading her by the path-
ways of theology back to the Trinity. And it sprang too from
a chance happening in her spiritual life. We recall that, from
the feast of the Ascension to Pentecost of the year 1623, she
was tormented by a spiritual night of anguish, in which her
understanding and her heart were darkened. From this trial
she was delivered on the feast of Pentecost by an infusion of
the Holy Spirit, and by the gift of his graces of light and
strength. She was healed, or to use a better expression, she
was conquered. Henceforward, the anniversary of this day
was sacred to her. Every year, at Ascensiontide, she went
into retreat to prepare herself to receive the Holy Spirit.
She spent ten days in union and communion with the
Apostles. It was a waiting period, at once quiet and active,
in which she prepared her soul to receive a great visitor. She
used the time to remove from mind and heart every obstacle
that could oppose his coming, or his full possession upon
arrival—not only sin, but every attachment that was not to
God, and—note this carefully—every attachment to spiritual
consolations, which the Presence of Jesus Christ brings with
it. Louise took literally the mysterious text of St John xvi,

7-11, where Jesus, taking leave of his disciples, told them he was leaving because of his love for them: 'But I tell you the truth: it is expedient to you that I go: for if I go not, the Paraclete will not come to you; but if I go, I will send him to you. And when he is come, he will convince the world of sin, and of justice, and of judgment. Of sin: because they believed not in me. And of justice: because I go to the Father; and you shall see me no longer. And of judgment: because the price of this world is already judged. I have yet many things to say to you: but you cannot bear them now. But when he, the Spirit of truth, is come, he will teach you all truth.' Louise's reaction to these words was remarkable: to receive the Spirit, we must be totally detached from all which is not Jesus Christ, 'and even from the tendernesses of his presence, so that, our soul being empty of all the hindrances which could present an obstacle to him, the Divine Spirit can fill it'. In one of her hours of elation, when she was caught up by the love of Christ, she had said to him: 'Take away from me your consolations and your tenderness, for I desire but you alone.' But now she said to him, trembling, 'Withdraw yourself, leave me empty and alone, for you have said that you must leave me for the Spirit to take possession of me'. Here is a singular development, when mystical asceticism goes so far as to deny itself love and the Divine Presence.

When the Spirit had thus taken hold of a soul, provided it does not resist his activity, he will do great things in it and for it. If we want to know what these great things are, we only have to consider the power of his gifts and the transformation which each one of them could work in us. And Louise, the moral theologian, takes this view of the mystery of the predestined: she holds that the obvious differences between one man and another arise from the varying use which each one makes of the Gifts of the Spirit: understanding, counsel, wisdom, strength.... These gifts strengthen our Christian life. They give vitality to the Mystical Body of the Church, and make of us witnesses to Christ in a world which knows him not.

This lofty doctrine was not just an idea but a conviction of her mind and heart. It became part of herself and whenever she wrote, whenever she prayed, she referred to 'the Spirit' as other spiritual writers refer to God or to Jesus Christ. More precisely, her thought tended always towards the Trinity and most willingly towards the Third Person, as towards that love which would make her worthy of the Father by making her more like the Son. This preoccupation absorbed her even at the moment of Communion. She clearly saw that the Communion is food, and that the purpose of food is that it should transform our substance. She besought the Holy Spirit, before and after Communion, that this transformation might take place in her, so that she might come to resemble him by whom she was fed. I care very little for the high-sounding terminology of science; but spiritual writers speak of theocentric and christocentric souls. I venture to use the word 'pneumatocentric', to characterise the spirituality of Louise de Marillac. She is the disciple of the Holy Ghost. She is the mystic of the Holy Ghost. Let me quote here a short saying: 'The Spirit who fills us with the pure love of God. . . . The Spirit makes us obedient to God, so that we may share the divine life.'

This raises another question. Can it be said that Louise de Marillac was a mystic? If so, she came to mysticism by a spiritual way, whose stages we must now mark out.

THE STAGES IN HER SPIRITUAL COURSE

THE EDITORS of the four-volume private edition of the writings of Louise de Marillac were confronted with a problem very difficult of solution, but of which they well understood the importance.

Many of her letters are not dated; her meditations and thoughts are never dated; this is a serious drawback when one wishes to use them in a study of her spiritual development. We propose to base our remarks upon the provisional classifications adopted by the editors, and to give special attention to papers which may be assigned to five decisive periods in the life of Louise. As indicated by all her biographers, these years are 1623, 1629, 1644 and 1651. These dates need not be rigorously adhered to: they are simply times when feelings, resolutions, and the effects of grace converge.

On the feast of Pentecost, 1623, she had been delivered by the Holy Spirit from a condition of neurasthenia, due to a long series of trials which arose out of the circumstances of her birth. Psychologists may attempt to determine the nature and the causes of this malady by comparing it to similar cases of psychic disorder; but in the supernatural order, this was probably also one of those severe trials or temptations to which reference is made in the Our Father, a crisis in which a Christian stands with his back to the wall, a trial similar to the one which began the ministry of our Lord. From this trial she did not emerge to enter into the fullness of divine peace, for she still had no strength, no capacity to take the right road, no idea how to do so. She fell back again upon herself, no doubt a little closer to God, yet in a colloquy somewhat limited, in which her powers could only find employment in a love of God still largely selfish. This

THE STAGES IN HER SPIRITUAL COURSE

imperfect love, which suffered from a knowledge of its own imperfection, drove her to raise herself up by following the lessons and example of Vincent de Paul and giving herself to the relief of the poor.

It was thus that, by 1629, she had begun the ascent of the holy mountain; as she herself said, she went to God by means of others.

This next stage, like all those which follow, began with a retreat, in strictly classic form laid down by her director. He induced her to rely once more upon herself, and as it were try out her working tools, before undertaking a labour which would draw her out and away from herself and give to her love for God a source of nourishment external to herself. During the next four or five years, with an astonishing strength, she co-operated in this expanding life of love. Thus she found herself on the right road; it is in the love of others that God is most truly found; and it was her vocation to find God in such love. It only remained that she should be fixed and settled in the right way by some precise undertaking or commitment of herself, to which she could give the form of that vow of religion which in earlier days she had so earnestly desired and attempted, and which had then tormented her for years after, because she believed she had broken her word. This was the stage which centred around the year 1634. It corresponded to her entering religion. Henceforth she was no longer seeking. She had completely broken with what we call 'the world'.

It is noteworthy that during this stage—and, for the matter of that, in the succeeding stage also—just when she was pressing forward so eagerly towards the accomplishment of love, it was as if her path were rhythmically punctuated by the blows of suffering; the illnesses which attacked her delicate body, the anxieties caused by the escapades of her son, the tragic events which distracted her father's family, and the anxious scruples welling up from a conscience never entirely at rest. The consequent suffering was mingled, as her director expressed it, with the caresses of God, with the resulting bitter-sweetness which is the true flavour of Christian perfection.

Between 1634 and 1644 she reached full spiritual development and bloom. Delivered from her hesitations, sure of her way, for she had entered upon it under the care of a guide sent to her by God, she was able to bring all her powers into play for the service of God in the persons of God's poor.

Now at last she was borne along by grace and by the action of grace, though still liable to overwhelming attacks of spiritual anxiety. Her fundamental humility still sometimes brought her to the brink of despair, as when she had to stand by and see all her efforts thwarted by the rough pressure of worldly interests. But this was only by the way. The important thing, not very much in evidence, was the establishment and triumph of her personality, which was to achieve much that was new in the domain of charity and lend its colour to her inner life. She became increasingly aware of this, though she did not dare say so even when the house at Nantes was founded. On that memorable day she felt the joy of working in full accord with the promptings of grace and of being strong enough for her work, which would achieve something real and lasting for the poor. To have come so far was a considerable achievement, and it would rank in the eyes of the world as a new glory in the annals of a great family. It would be entered by God to the credit of a staunch Christian woman, whose love had borne fruit.

On the supernatural plane, where things are not measured to human scale, there is something nobler than the high eminence of the Marillac family; there is renunciation, the resolve to forgo grandeur, and sacrifice, the annihilation of everything that goes to make earthly greatness, the sacrifice of *all*, even if the gold be pure. I had almost said that, having attained a summit, Louise de Marillac turned right-about and began to descend again into abnegation and self-destruction. But to put it this way is still to measure by human values. To strip oneself, to deny oneself, to annihilate oneself, is not to descend; it is a process of self-emptying, a shedding of loads, so as to rise ever higher towards summits inaccessible to him who is bowed down by the weight of his own humanity.

For Louise, this flight to new renunciations began with a Pentecost retreat in 1643 or 1644, when she was suffering from shock following on the collapse of the floor at the mother-house. She herself noted the significance of this event in her spiritual life: it was a sign, a warning that God was especially concerned for her, and therefore expected of her some special offering, and not just the works of a love which showed itself in charitable deeds.

In the course of this retreat, the theme of her meditations was Jesus in his Mother's womb. There, he was most intimately united with our human nature; he was one with it, in virtue of a fleshly continuity of our flesh with his own. Louise gave much thought to this hidden state of the Son of God, and tells us that she received singular graces, by which she means, I suppose, moments of pure and divine love. Ever practical, she drew from these graces the following conclusion: 'I have to learn to stay continually hidden in God, in the desire to serve him, without seeking any more the approbation of creatures, or my own satisfaction in communication with others; being content that God should know that I desire to be his'.

This was confession. In the past she had been gratified by the general approval of her activity, and she had taken delight—which was certainly legitimate—in conversation with like-minded persons, with her Daughters, with Monsieur Vincent, with the Ladies. All this she now undertook utterly to renounce, that she might dwell alone with God only. This was the beginning of abnegation.

She was conscious forthwith that this form of self-denial is a painful exercise. She desired to be forgotten by her fellow-creatures—yet when they passed her by, she would be hurt.

It even seemed to her that it was unjust when she was ignored; no one understood her: 'Formerly, I did not like it when others took the credit for something I thought I had done myself.' This remark is an admission of a secret wound. The Ladies did their work in their own way, not with ostentation, but drawing up generous plans, which could not but bring their activities into the limelight, though the execution of these plans was left, as often as not, to Mademoiselle and her Daughters. In the eyes of the world and perhaps in their own sight the Ladies obtained prestige for the idea and merit for the result. Louise, who knew what the scheme had cost in terms of day-to-day toil, had no desire to make her share in it known, but she was not pleased that the credit should go elsewhere. Now, however, by a most grievous effort, she renounced all desire to keep account of the distribution of merit and effort, provided God was served. So long as God knew that Louise had desired to serve him for himself alone, what did all the rest matter?

There was one sphere in which she was unique, and need not fear that any one else would claim the credit: this was the direction of her Daughters. We know with what love and passionate watchfulness she devoted herself to their formation and daily direction. In leadership that is inspired by reason and the desire for the good, and that is acceptable to subordinates, there is a very subtle joy. The best and most disinterested of men and women cannot but be conscious of it, and Louise had certainly relished it to the full, looking upon it as a gift from God. She renounced it now—and she must have found it difficult to do so, since, unable to give up her command, she could not prevent herself finding joy in it. She does, however, record some little progress along this road: 'I may say that I have renounced the ambition to be a leader.' She continued to lead, as a matter of duty—and we now begin to understand what is meant by interior abnegation.

This self-abnegation of hers extended to every part of her

life. We have already noticed some of its manifestations. She renounced her dominating love for her son and schooled herself to treat him as she would any other child of God. She renounced certain prayers and pious habits to which she had been much attached. She felt that in this way she was advancing towards God, and that grace was inviting her to quicken her step. Searching for words to express what she felt, but falteringly, as if she scarcely dared claim that she was making progress, she wrote to Monsieur Vincent: 'I feel within me an indescribable disposition, by which, as it seems, I desire to draw near to God, but I know not how to do it.'

In this new way, which she had entered with the sanction of her director, she felt the difficulties which are inherent in such an advance, when considered in conjunction with the external activities in which she was engaged. At the very moment when she was absorbed in her work of spiritual denudation, someone would pluck her by the sleeve to say that the *Enfant Trouvés* had not a scrap of bread left in the house, or that Sister Marie had done something silly. This was during the Pentecost retreat of 1647. But now, and this was a new feature in her character, she found herself absorbing all these daily difficulties and being nourished by them: she built them into the framework of her abnegations. In a letter to Vincent de Paul, she said:

'I believe God does not wish me to taste his sweetness to the full. I have reason to confess, and I acknowledge, that I do nothing of any value. My heart is not becoming embittered on this account, although there is reason to fear that the mercy of God may grow weary of pouring itself out on a creature who so regularly displeases him.'

She was not embittered, she was not complaining. She accepted the will of God, even though it seemed to be turning her away from him. She had stripped herself of spiritual impatience.

She began again, for she was always having to begin

again; and as she did so, she could remark that she had made
a little real progress, and that from now on she might look
upon certain weaknesses as done with for ever. On the
Ascension Day of her 1649 retreat, she realised that, at the
moment of his triumph as he ascended to glory, Jesus declared
that he was still under obedience, as he had always been.

'What has caused me so much confusion is, that
formerly I was very much vexed that other people should
take the credit for work I thought I had done myself.
I have renewed a resolution which I have often made,
that I will not trouble myself, but let people believe what
they will, provided that God be served, no matter by
whom.'

She also understood as though by direct revelation that
Jesus, in his obedience to his Father, showed in his life a true
union of the life of action with the life of prayer. So the
spirit of detachment by which she feels herself to be beset
and almost absorbed could be reconciled with her active
service to the sick poor and to the servants of the sick poor.
There was in her a most true love of God, which previously
she had had to renew from time to time by positive contacts
and concrete acts; now, this love had become a state, under-
lying all she did, which would effect her total abnegation
without upsetting her active life. It was about the year
1651 that she entered upon this accelerated detachment, and
she did it, as usual, in her Pentecost retreat, of which the
plan was drawn up by Monsieur Vincent. One of her biographers, Collet, has given us a *résumé* of this retreat, though
without quoting his authority. The new features in this plan
of retreat seem to be as follows: the retreatant passed very
rapidly through the exercises of the purgative and the
illuminative way, the secrets of both of which she well
knew, to reach the stage of abandonment to God and deliver
herself to him to do his will with her. From this point, she
no longer had control of the retreat: it was God who guided
her. The director and the retreatant were of too great a

humility to suppose that they could thus enter the way of mystical union; but the fact is that they had arrived at it, and we shall shortly see that Louise de Marillac made further progress along it. For the moment she believed that her abnegations should still be related to external things, that she would go on and achieve her detachment in this way, yet in reality she was already at work on interior detachment.

'I do not hear that the kingdom of Heaven lies in anything other than thyself, O my God! What then? Thou belongest to those who possess nothing. O truly, thou art the only All! To have thee, I desire to renounce all things. O, pure Love, how I love thee! Thou art strong as death! Separate me from all things contrary to thee!'

All those things which create obstacles to pure love because they form no part of him, she stubbornly enumerates, probing into the remotest recesses of her being. She begins by rejecting her very being, as a whole and totally: 'I desire to be absolutely extinguished by the annihilation of my whole inner life.' Here we have a genuine realisation of mystic union. But these are only words, and must be put into practice.

She fell back upon the graces she had received; and here we begin to understand that she must indeed have been almost encumbered with graces, so frequently does she mention them. Now she asks that they be taken away, that she be delivered from them—she wants God only. But God caused her to understand that she had not received them for herself alone. She then began to grasp the meaning of one of Vincent de Paul's golden rules: that she was but an instrument in the hands of God, the hatchet in the hands of the woodcutter, the reed in the hands of the basket-maker. This was to be the summing-up of her own personality, and she accepted the verdict. 'I ask of God that he should not subsist in me.'

God alone *is*. She was never to forget the revelation received in one of her retreats. She had been troubled by a page in the *Memorial* of Luis of Granada, which spoke of predestination; and she received her consolation when she read, in the same author's *Guide*, that God is he who *is*. She had not been unaware of it, but now she understood it as truth, and laid hold of it for ever. Because of this, she could hope to lose her own being in the Being of God. But, as though alarmed at the ambition of her desire, she cut it down to more humane and precise limits; to the essential sacrifice of her own liberty: 'Since I do not desire ownership in my freewill, I resign it into the hand of God, and of my director.'

It will be of interest to note the form taken by this detachment, this mystic procedure, when the Foundress came to apply it, as sooner or later she had to do, in the course of her duty in the direction of her Daughters. Writing in 1658 to Marguerite Chétif, one of the most advanced in spirituality, she said:

'I am not astonished that our Saviour has made you a partner in his interior sufferings. Would you have supposed yourself to be thus honoured before God and his angels, if the honour had cost you nothing? I have not the slightest doubt that his grace bears you up very strongly in your renunciations and your states of indifference. Do you not know, my dear Sister, that these are trials to which the holy Bridegroom of our souls takes his delight, when they are used with loving patience and tranquil acquiescence, without falling into scruple about what we suffer when we are in such a state? I know well that you are careful not to lose these occasions of showing your fidelity, and that your heart will never allow itself to listen to the reasonings of the natural sense, which cause us to look at things from outside the control of Divine Providence, and as though they were not the accomplishment of the most holy will of God.

'I know also that you will turn a deaf ear to any mourning for the garlic and onions of Egypt, to any

desire for the satisfaction of being in one's own homeland and among one's acquaintance. These will sometimes speak us fair and seem to do us good, because our feelings are engaged and our minds take pleasure for a time in thinking of such things; but we do not in the end find that we are any the more virtuous for that. If we are being tried by mortification and temptation, we are at once defeated and in a deplorable state! And indeed, we should be so if we did not hold fast to God by a leaping forward of the mind, saying to him from the bottom of of our heart: My God! in all that pleases thee, I am thine! working all our actions, despite temptations, purely and simply for the love of God, contenting ourselves with what his will desires we should be, in that state in which he puts us, whether by the ordering of his own Providence or through his creatures.

'Have you never noted, my dear Sister, what we can learn from St John the Baptist, who knew and loved our Lord so well that he bore witness to him in the ways that you know? Yet the Baptist withdrew himself from our Lord, or rather God separated him from him, by his vocation to penance, although he had not been born in sin. Do you not think that God wished to give this example to those souls which he desires to separate from all earthly affections, that he may fill their hearts with holy love? What consolation, when a soul sees itself thus entirely dependent on his particular guidance! It is sufficient that I should rejoice with you in this dependence.'

The confidence is veiled, that it may come within the little Sister's range and grasp; but we can feel the loving vibration underneath the words.

TOWARDS MYSTICAL UNION

THE WORD 'mysticism' is often slipping from my pen. Yet I know that Vincent de Paul, dazzled by the radiance of Saint Teresa, thought himself unworthy to enter that world of reserved thought. Yet that was where he had directed Louise de Marillac, not by premeditated design, but in obedience to the movement of the Holy Spirit. During the closing years of her life, Louise entered into the mystical life, as defined by St Teresa: she experienced union with God in pure love and in the silence of the senses and of reason. To this union she was called by God himself, and especially in the course of her retreats, by mystical invitations which she recorded very frequently, with vivid regret that she had not the strength to record them in detail, or to convey any impression of their intensity. Her response to these calls was the simple desire to bring to realisation the intentions of God concerning her. Let us look at some of these texts.

Upon entering the mystic state she had to detach herself from her reason and from reasoning processes; but here her mode of renunciation was very much her own: very French, Salesian, as was natural in so devoted a disciple of St Francis, and perhaps also with a Cartesian element. Her method consisted of renouncing reason without a total rejection of the reasoning process. 'I believe that God is within me, and I desire no other forms of reasoning than those which he inspires in me.' Whatever of reason persists in her mystical life came, therefore, not of herself, but of God. Thus Louise was reassured—and we are warned.

It is not astonishing that she should be called into this way; it is not reserved to exceptional characters. 'All souls are called to the practice of pure love; when I shall have been lifted up from the earth, I will draw all men unto myself.' She

was attracted to that exalted place which is the hill of the
Cross, and when she entered upon the royal road of suffering
she did not at first realise that it was also the way of mystical
union. But she soon understood that 'to suffer and to love
are the same thing'. As I have said, we do not find in her
intimate writings that the daily suffering, moral and
physical, through which she passed held any redemptive
significance for her. She looked upon suffering simply as
suffering, and not for any use to which it might be put. Her
sorrow is a state of sharing in Christ's suffering; more than
that, of sharing in Christ's suffering and so in union with
him. In fact, sorrow was a treasure which she shared with
Christ crucified. That was enough for her, and she needed
no other thought or feeling than of suffering shared with
him. This is one of the higher forms of love, of that special
love which had been revealed to her on the feast of the Sacred
Heart. She says that on this day she received 'I know not
what new light on a love which is not common, and which
you desire from those human hearts which you invite, to
exalt upon earth the purity of your charity'. She sought words
and images with which to express this very uncommon love;
her humility did not dare to affirm that God was enriching
her in any continuous way. She was not worthy of such a
love, yet it was not for her to refuse, since the love had already
been given.

> 'It has seemed to me that God desired to come to
> me as into a place which is his own, and that therefore I
> could not refuse to admit him, which would moreover
> have been quite impossible for me, since I had already
> once and for all put into his hands the proprietorship of
> my free will.'

God was then sole Master within her. As I have said, she
retained in her mystical life the use of her reason, reason
bestowed on her by God, and she made use of it to conclude:
'I ought then to desire to die, but if I consent to go on living,
let it be a life of love. How can I not flow into this ocean of
G

your love?' Elsewhere, returning to expressions which are
dear to her, she longed to absorb her being into the Being of
God. Taking her stand once more upon the earth, and
knowing well that the earth still held her, she went so far as
to offer the prayer: 'May the use of my senses be weakened'.
We must tremble before the sincerity of a woman who knew
the value and force of words and never misused them; she
was asking that her use of her own senses, sight, hearing, all
the organs of her life on earth, might be weakened. All this
was to be to the advantage of a life of another kind, which
had already begun in her. Louise was always most discreet
and measured in her use of words, yet she dared to describe
this higher life: when we are liberated from all attachment
to this world and to the senses, from all attachment to our
own self-love and our own freewill, and even from attachment to the sweetnesses of Christ and to his presence, when
we have created within ourselves a complete void, the Holy
Spirit will come into it and make us live with a life that is
divine.

A word of caution. Spiritual writers, or rather, the writers
of books on spirituality, have accustomed us to the use of
previous metaphors to such an extent that their distinctive
shades of meaning, if they ever had any such, have become
completely lost. For example, they speak of living with the
Life Divine as an ideal at which we ought to aim, but they
do not make clear what is the nature of this life, nor what are
its conditions, nor the time required to attain to it. But in
the present case there can be no doubt that we are dealing
with a real experience. For brief moments Louise de Marillac
attained to mystical union, and consequently participated in
the Life Divine. She was a saint, a holy one, *sancta*.

This life of union with the Spirit, the Life Divine, she lived
in the midst of every kind of turmoil, in face of her poor
health, without lessening her activity for her Daughters and
her ministrations to the poor. And then, little by little, her
environment began to change. The conditions of her daily

life were transformed, and what had formerly been a sorrowful and meritorious offering to the Love of God became an element in that Love, and as it were the substance of it. She had carried her Daughters in her heart, trained them and transformed them, loved them that her love might transform them, loved them the more as she watched them grow in grace—and very naturally she had loved them as her own handiwork. Now, and in proportion as she approached the apogee of her own ascetic course, the expression of her tenderness, while still vivid, lent more to nature. Her Daughters were no longer the cherished girls to whom she was individually attached, to one for her vivacity, to another for her meekness, to this other for her very faults. But all were now incorporated into a true mystical body, moving forward to meet the Spirit, and she loved them for the work of detachment upon which, as a community and as individuals, they had embarked, so that the entire Congregation, like its Foundress, might hope one day to arrive at union with the Spirit. The day might be distant, but now it would certainly come. All of us are called to the life of mystical union: we are called as individuals, and we are also called as groups.

The poor, too, were integrated into the life of union as experienced by the Foundress. Like her director and spiritual father, she entered deeply into the mysticism of material poverty. The poor are our masters, our princes and rulers, because in the mystical sense they are the Poor Christ. The more closely we are united with them and with their poverty, the more closely are we joined with the poverty of Christ and with Christ himself. Between Vincent de Paul and Louise de Marillac there was complete agreement in thought, feeling and accent, but it is curious to note that they arrived at this *mystique* of the poor in different ways.

Louise de Marillac was an aristocrat by birth and an intellectual by tendency. She sought out the poor as a Christian duty, even though the duty should be a hard service even to the end. In her contacts with the poor she discovered a human warmth which perhaps she hardly expected, and she loved them as part of humanity, though she was still the great lady intent upon her duty. But Christian doctrine, touched and transformed by the Vincentian fire, transformed her ordinary human attitudes.

Vincent de Paul, on the other hand, was of peasant origin, and concrete by tendency. He did not have to go to the poor, or seek them out. He was one of them, and between his soul and theirs there was an affinity. He loved them spontaneously because he and they were, humanly speaking, one. Since he was a Christian, it was in them that he found the image of God, and God himself.

These formulas are, of course, over-simplified, and not absolutely just. Yet we may venture to say that, while Vincent went to God as he found him in the poor, Louise went to the poor by God and through God. The result is the same: when they speak of the poor, the terms they use are the same terms. But there is a slight variation in tone, which we can discern if we put ourselves in the place of one of the poor, who would have liked, had he dared, to take his brother's hand in his, but to kiss the hand of the great lady.

We have come now to 1658-1659. The general impression now is that the external details of Louise's life had all been subordinated to her interior life, and that they were now, from day to day, being transformed into that unique spiritual offering which she made to the Holy Spirit in her union with him: This was her work of love, and it was a love which was dramatic in character, for it was uncertain and always threatened from without, and it was always in need of external support. Such was the contradictory nature, and the limitations, of a mystical life which burned, which was devoured, with ardent love.

This woman had suffered too much, she had been too much pounded and bruised throughout her childhood, too deeply wounded in the depths of her personality; and it is little wonder that to the end of her days she was fearful when memory rose up to haunt her. An exact sense of sin and of the weakness of human nature nourished in her an anxiety which was a permanent factor in her makeup, and which is indeed a familiar experience of even the most balanced characters. Hence the periodical assaults upon this soul, otherwise so sturdy, of astonishing alarms and paralysing fears which made her a child again, a scared child in need of comfort and reassurance. A few words would suffice to calm the storm, but she could not do without those words: ten minutes talk with him who knew the secrets of peace. Without her director, all would have been lost: she had no idea what she would do, she would have to appear before God in a state of inexpressible confusion.

The time had come when Mademoiselle could no longer go out of doors very much; and since Vincent de Paul also scarcely ever left his chamber, Louise was deprived of his society and his strong support.

The situation became tense. She wrote:

'Also tomorrow is the 25th of the month [of July], on which day there should be said the Holy Mass for the whole Company, for the needs and intentions which your charity knows.

'Permit me, my much honoured Father, to tell you that my powerlessness to do any good prevents me from having any pleasing thing to offer to our Saviour, apart from my miserable renewal, except the privation of the only consolation which his goodness has granted me in thirty-five years. I accept this for love of him, in the manner which his providence ordains, hoping of his goodness and your charity one and the same help by an interior way, and I ask it of you, for the love of the union of the Son of God with human nature, without losing hope, however, of seeing you when that shall be possible without harm to the little health which God has given you. I beg of him to preserve it to you, until the entire accomplishment of his purposes for your soul, to his glory and for the benefit of several others, of whom I have the honour to be one.'

It is necessary to hear out to the end that plaintive voice, the voice of a woman most pathetic in her weakness. She spoke of it to none but the Father, and perhaps that was why she was sometimes so depressed. To her Daughters she showed her other side: her awareness and her peace. We should read her last letter, written to one of her beloved Daughters. It is so tranquil, so tranquillising, so full of gentle expressions, that it seems to come from out of another world.

'I do not doubt that you have a great deal to do, nor also that you take great care to help our Sisters to work at their perfection. Please always to send me news of them, I beg, and tell me especially if, while engaged in external serving, their interior consciousness is engaged, for the love of our Lord, in watchfulness over themselves, to conquer their passions and suppress them, refusing their senses anything which could cause them to give offence to God. Without this interior vigilance, you know that external acts cannot give great pleasure to God, nor merit reward for us, since they are not united with those of our Lord, whose work was always done in the presence of his Father. You are well versed in his way, my dear Sister, and you therefore experience the peace of a soul which leans in this way upon its Well-Beloved.'

Then came the end. At the beginning of February, 1660, she lay for six weeks completely prostrated by her illness. It cannot be said that she was in her agony, for there was no active struggle with death, but she was remote from all that we call life. She herself conducted this detachment in fitting order. First, she took leave of her children: her son, her daughter-in-law, her grandchild, and gave them her blessing. Then she said farewell to the community, and to the Sisters who were waiting on her, to those who were distant, thinking of her; she gave her blessing to them, bidding them be faithful to their vocation, insisting repeatedly

that she died in the love of her own vocation to the service
of the sick and the poor for the love of God. That was all.
Then, with only the duchesse de Ventadour to watch over
her, she could believe that she was at last alone.

A last trial now exercised her heart. Before her departure,
was she not to have the consolation of seeing for a moment
him who for thirty-seven years had sustained her, and whom
she very dearly loved? He was but two paces away from her,
on the other side of the street. To be sure, Vincent de Paul
was now himself so worn out and weak that his legs could
scarcely carry him. But at the hour of her death, would he
not endeavour once more the impossible, to give encouragement to her whom he had encouraged so long and loved so
dearly? She asked for Monsieur Vincent—and Monsieur
Vincent sent no reply. Schooled now in sacrifice, Louise
renounced this last desire, renounced the visit which would
have been very sweet to her before the last closing of her eyes.
Yet, if he could not come, let him but write her a word or
two, one of those little austere and tender letters with which
he had so many times consoled her.

Monsieur Vincent refused. He sent a Brother to tell the
sick woman she should depart in peace, and that before very
long he would join her. This farewell by proxy had cost him
as much as it cost her. The frigidity of it fills us with amaze-
ment. But it was necessary that detachment should be
complete. The dying woman accepted.

Now, she had given everything.

And yet, it was not so. She had not yet given everything.
She was resigned to not hearing from him, she was content
not to read any consoling message; but she had not consented
no longer to love him. Our literature and art, our mortal
baseness, have so cheapened all the expressions of tenderness
and love that we now use them with the utmost trepidation.
Yet they belong to us as part of our language, and we have
a right to make use of them, just as did Christ our Lord
himself. Louise de Marillac had surrendered everything.

There remained to her only this one precious stone which was enshrined in her heart: her love. Years ago, in many a conversation with the holy Jane de Chantal, a great many secrets must have been divulged, a great many intimacies must have been shared. Madame de Chantal may have told her how, two years before he died, Francis de Sales had asked his dear daughter to make the sacrifice of her love for him, as he would similarly sacrifice his feeling for her. And she had obeyed. This was a drama played out upon the heights, and such struggles are sometimes more bloody, and always more noble, than those of human life, and of art.

If Jane de Chantal did indeed so confide in Louise de Marillac, then Mademoiselle knew the way she had to take. She too could make this final offering: and so her heart was emptied of all love, of all loves, even the noblest and the purest. She was without the consolations from her spiritual Father, and without consolation from Christ. Complete emptiness. This was the hour for the Spirit to lay hold of the heart thus painfully prepared to receive him, and to fill it entirely. The mystical union was complete.

And so occurred for Louise de Marillac the event we know as death. We may even note the date of it: March 15th, 1660. But we are wrong to regard death as an ending. The death of the saints is a continuation, and even a fixed state of continued life. While the earthly body goes through with its own adventure, in corruption and disintegration, dust to dust, until at the resurrection it is remade, the soul united to the Holy Spirit continues its life along a course that is already fixed for ever. Death simply marks its expansion. As we stand at the deathbed of Louise de Marillac, with tears and prayers about us, this is the reality, the only thing that matters. Those who judge as mortals do or pass by as quickly as they can, as though these details bored them, or find the cruelties of the saints very hard to bear and understand, will be led back to the truth by the words of Vincent de Paul. In the conference at which he presided which followed Louise's death, he said very simply, mastering his own emotion, that he had been deprived of the consolation of seeing the dying woman again, and that Providence had willed this for her perfection. This is the word that must endure. That death, crowning so many sacrifices, was an achievement, a perfection.

There is nothing consistent about the metaphors we habitually use, giving no thought to their origin. It is said that with the memory of the dead, and particularly of the saints, there is mingled the perfume of their virtues. Pious legend, turning a metaphor into fact, declares that from the tombs of some of the dead a persistent perfume does indeed arise.

The Abbé Gobillon, who was an intelligent and loyal man, declared at the process for the beatification of Vincent de Paul that after the death of Louise de Marillac, and for a long time thereafter, he noticed a particular perfume about her tomb. He observed that the Sisters who came to visit the tomb also noticed this perfume, carrying it away upon their habits, and spreading it about the sickrooms where they worked. Who can say what degree of simplicity and purity of heart is required, before the spiritual perfume can be noticed? However this may be, the perfume which emerged from a tomb that was glorious, mingled with the gloom that once enveloped an anxious cradle. Within this mystery, the meaning of which we cannot know, unfolds the paradox of a holiness which is acceptable to God, a holiness which defied the world for the world's confusion, and for its own salvation.

APPENDIX

Details of the careers of members of the Marillac family.

The careers of Michel de Marillac and Louise, Comte de Beaumont, held glory, but also great misfortune.

We are told that *Michel* was a mystic, melancholy, passionate and impetuous. At the age of twenty-two he was Advocate to the *Parlement* and Master of Pleas. He threw himself, with passionate religious conviction, into the adventure of the League, and his courage gained for him the post of Advocate General to a new *Parlement*, purged of its Huguenot elements. When le Béarnais became a Catholic, Michel was sufficiently agile and practical to follow his conscience and prevail upon his colleague to open the gates of Paris to the King of Navarre. Michel was a favourite of the queen, Marie de Medici, as well as of Richelieu, so that his rise to power was continuous and led him leisurely upwards towards the highest post in the state: first, superintendent of finances; chancellor in 1626; keeper of the Seals in 1630. His probity, his ability, and his capacity for work enabled him to wield a strong influence in public life.

There then occurred to Michel de Marillac the great and dangerous idea of reforming and unifying the law of France, and to this end he ordered and supervised the compilation of the legal code known as the 'Code Michau', and imposed it by royal consent. Those who had long profited by the old abuses of the Law did not forgive him this forward step.

His absolute devotion to Marie de Medici, his attachment to his half-brother, Louis, the Marshal, and his personal ambition drew Michel into a conspiracy against Richelieu—a conspiracy which very nearly succeeded. For forty-eight hours in November 1630 Michel was actually the King's first minister of state, in place of the Cardinal. But Richelieu returned to power, and clapped the ephemeral minister into prison. It was the end of Michel's public life and he found it hard to resign himself to this stroke of fortune, but he never ceased to be a man of prayer, and now his faith restored him to stability in the midst of his troubles. In his prison at Châteaudun, this man, who was both Christian scholar and political intriguer, absorbed himself in translating into French the Penitential Psalms and the *Imitation of Christ*. The teaching he drew from these texts sustained his courage. He died in 1632, a Frenchman in the grand manner, enigmatic by reason of the contradictory elements, which are really no more than contrasts, in his character.

His half-brother, *Louis*, comte de Beaumont, was a man of a different stamp. Handsomest of all the Marillacs—and all were famed for their good looks—he followed the profession of arms, though with audacity rather than competence. He was a dare-devil captain of light horse, and this good-looking, bold young man soon began to make conquests in the highest quarters. It was not long before he attracted the notice of Catherine de' Medici, daughter of Duke Cosimo and aunt of Queen Marie. With a king for witness, he married Catherine in the Louvre. The way was at once opened for the entire Marillac family to be received into royal favour, and to be given some of the highest posts in the state. The Marillacs therefore began to move with great resolution into the orbit of the Queen, ranging themselves with those Italian families already in possession and acquiring a name for themselves—the Cocini, the Gondi, and many another.

Louis Marillac de Beaumont had a share in all the campaigns, and though envied for his growing influence at Court, he was sustained by his courage, and in the end betrayed by his own imprudence and the Marillac ambition. It began to be whispered that he was in secret correspondence with the Queen his niece, Marie de Medici, and was conspiring against Richelieu, whom she detested. It was true.

On his return to power, Richelieu had Louis de Beaumont arrested in Italy, where he was serving. His trial began, inspired by personal hatred and political intrigue. He defended himself with bitterness. He was charged with speculation and misappropriation of the public funds. His hands were certainly not clean, yet such faults were very common ones in his profession. He was condemned and beheaded in the Place de Grève. The affair made a great stir. Windows were rented for a view of the handsome Marshal's death, and a hundred thousand people were present at his execution. But when Richelieu died, Marillac de Beaumont was solemnly rehabilitated by the *Parlement* of Paris. He was, like his brother Michel, a Frenchman in the grand manner.

Valence de Marillac, sister of the Marshal, was beautiful. In 1598 she married Octavin Doni d'Attichy, a man highly esteemed at Court who became superintendent of Finances to Marie de Medici. Doni d'Attichy died young, leaving his widow with five children.